7

BLUE SKIES and TAIL WINDS

by

Captain Dana L. VanLoan

Sunnyside Press
St. Johnsville, New York   Berkeley, California

BLUE SKIES and TAIL WINDS

Library of Congress Cataloging-in-Publication Data

Van Loan, Dana L. , 1953-
  Blue skies and tail winds / by Dana L. Van Loan
      p. cm.
  Summary: "Presents stories describing author's experiences from
1990-2005 during his mid-life career change from dairy agricul-
ture to aviation, first as a private pilot, then as pilot of an air
ambulance, and finally as Captain-in-Command of Lear jets for
corporate avaiation"--Provided by publisher.
    ISBN 0-9717214-1-6 (alk. paper)
  1. Van Loan, Dana L. , 1953- 2. Air pilots--United States--
Biography. 3. Private flying--United States. I. Title

TL540.V322.A3 2005
629.13'092--dc22

Printed and bound in the USA

SUNNYSIDE PRESS
St. Johnsville, New York   Berkeley, California

This book is dedicated to my wife,
Kathy Van Loan

BLUE SKIES and TAIL WINDS

CONTENTS

INTRODUCTION

Blue Skies and Tailwinds by Captain Dana L. Van Loan is a marvelous recollection of flying experiences written from a pilot's perspective by a one time dairyman who changed occupations midway through his working life and became a professional aviator. This collection of experiences is a must for the adventurer as well as for the aviation enthusiast. Dana has flown my family and I for several years through all kinds of weather and we have always felt safe while under his watch."

—Tom Brokaw

1. How It All Began

The year was 1942 and my Dad walked from his high school graduation ceremonies in Coxsackie, N.Y. with diploma in hand into the grasps of the United States Navy. For the next three years and 1,000 flight hours he was trained to be a Naval fighter pilot in the midst of the WWII conflict. As his deployment day was nearing and as he awaited his pressurized flight suit to arrive, the war ended.

Mom took her high school diploma in hand to Albany Business College and graduated from there a year later with a degree in business. She was hired soon after back in our home town of Fort Plain, New York as a business secretary at the local GLF feed store. Somehow on a blind date these two met and as they say the rest is history. I know two things for sure; if they hadn't met or had the war not ended when it did, I probably would not be here telling you these stories. Janet Waner Swarts and Grant William Van Loan were married on June 8, 1948 and settled on her family's small dairy farm consisting of 32 Holstein dairy cows with around 120 acres of cropland to feed the herd. In the spring of 1950 my sister Lynn Mary came along and 35 months later I came along. Lynnie and I had a great upbringing living the good and healthy hard working country life on the small but prosperous dairy farm . Life was grand. I would not have traded it for anything with anyone. I graduated from high school in 1971 and went on to Cornell University enrolled in a special one year agricultural program, then returned home to help run the family farm. For the next 22 years I was a dairyman working daily alongside Mom, Dad , Kathy my wife, Stephanie our daughter and sons, Ian and Jesse. The pay was poor but life was grand and rewarding. Again, I would not have traded any of these times for any thing else in this world.

Dad was always airplane crazy . Undoubtedly he inherited this from his dad who was quite a remarkable aviator back in the early days of aviation. My grandfather Van Loan served in WWI as a radio reconnaissance operator in hot air balloons and biplanes; he was trained to fly high above enemy lines to observe what was going on in the trenches below and radio back to headquarters what he saw. After WWI ended, my grandfather actually built one of the first homebuilt aircraft ever, a Heath Parasol, right in his own shop, by hand, using a small 25 horsepower Henderson motorcycle engine for power.

Anyway, back to Dad. He would subscribe to and read those monthly magazines like Private Pilot, Flying, and Plane and Pilot as well as attending many of the local air shows as well as the granddaddy of them all, Oshkosh. I was always sort of exposed to the airplane environment but never really understood too much about planes and besides, how could

dairymen possibly have any extra time for those flying
machines when our noses were held to the farming
grindstone every day? I think Dad would have been perfectly
happy flying every day of his life, but after marrying and
starting a family he never really flew much after that. It
wasn't until I was 38 years old that something happened
within me .

One day I wanted to fly over the farm and take some
pictures, so I went up the road about five miles to nearby
Ray Gould's place to beg for a ride. Raymond was also a
local country farm boy who had made the big times as an
Eastern Airlines Captain and had recently taken an early
retirement package from the financially stressed airline; he
had also recently purchased this 1946 Pa 11 Cub Special
from South Dakota. I'll never forget what happened next.
When I showed up and asked for a ride, Raymond was
talking with a neighbor and of course he said come on, hop
in my bright yellow cub, which I did. He told me to hold
the brakes while he was turning the propeller over by hand.
I remember thinking that the battery or starter must be bad
and, who knows, the whole plane might be bad, or not
airworthy for that matter. Little did I know that a battery
and starter would simply add a lot of extra weight to the
plane and performance would therefore suffer, and also little
did I realize that the next twenty minutes was going to
change my life forever.

Ray told me to move this thing called the mag switch
to the "both" position and the next flick of the prop brought
the machine roaring to life. We flew over my farm and I
remember dropping a handkerchief parachute out of the
plane to one of our hired man's kids below to catch. It was
only a twenty-minute flight, but I landed with my arteries
and veins full of the deadly yellow venom called flying fever.
I was hooked. I immediately began lessons at a run down

little local barnyard airport called Nellis Field. I began on Thanksgiving morning in 1990 and on Labor Day of 1991 I was an FAA certified private pilot.

My first 'passenger' was Mom. I remember being so nervous on the drive to the airport that I was sick to my stomach—what if the airplane motor quit? For the first time I had the life of another in the palm of my flying hand. The flight went well and Mom fell asleep part way through, so I figured my take offs and landings must be fairly good even though I was pretty new at this business of flying airplanes. I immediately began taking more lessons for my instrument license. I frequently spoke with Ray, and my instructor Ken Kamp, and they strongly suggested that furthering my training would increase both my proficiency and the chance to make this fun pastime thing a long-lived fun pastime thing. I received my instrument license two years later in the spring of 1993 and started thinking, and thinking, and thinking.

I was about to sell the cows as Mom and Dad wanted to retire. My daughter and two sons had no interest in the farm and I had come to a fork in the road of my life. I was 40 years old and had been a dairy and crop farmer for the only 22 working years of my life. What would I do for the next 22 years? I secretly held this idea in my head that maybe someday, somehow I would actually fly airplanes for a living, and even get paid for it! But then reality would set in and I'd say, nah, that could never happen to me, so I went about selling the family farm by myself, without a realtor involved; the arrangement being I was to work for the new owners doing what I had always done and raising crops on 500 acres and milking 110 cows twice a day, every day, even on Christmas and New Year's day and every other holiday, and did I mention twice each and every day no matter what? This was all I knew life to consist of, and to tell you the truth, after selling the farm and relieving myself of that half a million dollar load on my mind, I felt almost young again, and life once again was grand.

About six months after selling the farm the new owners said they couldn't seem to find the money that I was to be paid for my services and that I could go and find a job that would pay if I needed the money. Hello! Yes, I do indeed need money to survive, so I took a job doing veterinarian work at a nearby mega dairy farm where they were milking over 500 cows. I ran the sick cow barn, administering around 20 bottles of calcium and dextrose intravenously, every day, until winter set in. The barn had only a roof and no sides. I vividly remember Thanksgiving morning. It was15 degrees below zero with howling northwesterly winds and snow blowing into the pole barn where I was giving the IV bottles; finally I said to myself, I used to do this stuff in my own barn but I'll be danged if I'm going to do this crap for some body else, and in a barn that has no sidewalls, so I finished that day's medical work, thawed out my frozen fingers, then politely quit.

Two days later I was hired in a milk bottling plant as a clean-up man. I worked Mondays, Wednesdays and Fridays only and had four days off every week. It was now the dead of winter but by God I was warm and working inside. Not knowing what I could possibly do with all of these days off from work, I began taking Commercial Pilot flying lessons just for kicks and giggles. After a year of these I figured out if I could somehow pull all of these loose ends together and manage to pass a Commercial Pilot check ride, I could then become an instructor, or just give rides and actually be paid to fly! Even so, this was still just a wild dream that seemed unreal to me and also to everyone else that knew me. I had to bite the bullet and borrow three grand in order to finish my dream rating. Those high performance airplanes were as much to rent per hour with an instructor as I was grossing each week at the dairy. But somehow in the summer of 1995 I passed my check ride and was a certified commercial pilot in single engine airplanes, and with instrument privileges. Awesome ! I could finally fly for pay non-stop sight-seeing flights of no more than twenty miles away from home base.

I immediately started studying feverously for all of my instructor ratings. I suddenly realized that after coming this far, maybe—just maybe—I could turn this fun stuff into an occupation, in spite of a nagging voice of doubt.

A year later found me passing my flight instructor check ride and soon after that my instrument instructor check ride. I had a dream and son of a gun maybe, just maybe, it was going to all come together. Part way through all of this training my instructor Ken started flying Lear jets for a local air ambulance company that was just starting up. I had heard Raymond talk of *his* jets. Then I had heard Ken talk of *his* jets. Suddenly I knew I wanted to some day tell someone about *my* jets ! The seed had been sown. Now it was just a matter of more dedicated hard work and someday maybe, just maybe, I could be rewarded.

I started teaching people how to fly airplanes in 1997 and in two years had totaled over 2,000 hours, 400 as a pilot myself and 1,600 as a flight instructor. I had even sent in a resumé to Ken's employer but never thought anything would ever become of that possibility. For I was only flying 150s, 172s, 182s, 182RGs, 210s and occasionally 206s, Beech Bonanzas and Twin Piper Senecas. I was as happy a pilot as you could ever find.

Then came the call. It was on my 46th birthday around noontime. It was Don Jones from Air Response and he had an opening for a Lear jet first officer, and asked if I wanted the job. I turned ice cold and went into shock. I was very happy doing what I was doing. Gee, after all this, maybe I don't want to fly jets, or do I ? I was all confused until once again my wife straightened me out. She said it had always been my dream and to go for it, because If I didn't like it or couldn't cut it, I could always fall back to where I was now. I called Don back and said—Sure !

Ground school training began the next day and lasted for a few afternoons. I was still teaching as a flight instructor daily, and then studying nightly all these complicated jet systems. I thought you only had to know how to *fly* these things. Why do I need to know these complex systems so intimately I wondered ? About a week after ground school had started I had been teaching all day at Fulton County Airport when Jeff , a check airman for Air Response, called and said my check ride for Second-in-Command was to be tonight and to meet him at Air Response's Schenectady hangar at 10 p.m. I'll never forget this night as long as I live. We flew around low at 4,000 feet and slow as possible, like around 200 knots until I was sort of comfortable, and then Jeff pushed forward the 'go fast' levers adding another 15,000 or so horsepower and away we climbed towards Canada from Schenectady until we were level at 41,000 feet 14 minutes later.

After some air work he told me to perform an emergency descent: M-A-P-S-G (oxygen Masks on, Autopilot off, Power to idle thrust, Spoilers extended and landing Gear down. Pitch the nose initially about 15 degrees down and then pitch for 265 knots of indicated airspeed or Mach 0.83. I was scared to death of this attitude and remember telling Jeff that I was going to ease the pitch attitude some so that we did not overstress the airframe as it was really making some strange noises. Jeff said, "No way, keep her at 265 until we're at 12,000 feet." It was one of the few big time scares in my 2,200 hour flying career so far. After leveling at 12,000 feet I flew steep turns at 250

knots and did a few approach-to-landing stalls. After Jeff
was satisfied and I was now thoroughly in shock from my
first ever attempt to pilot a Lear 24, we headed to Albany
and proceeded to do instrument approaches, touch and goes,
missed approaches and go-arounds and the likes. I can
assure anyone right here and now that you've never felt a
higher high than that felt doing touch-and-goes in a lightly
loaded Lear 24. Climb rates can easily exceed 10,000 feet
per minute, and any loose articles in the plane will all be
found in the rear cabin corners when the flight is finished.

Four hours after we started I was driving back toward
home on the New York State Thruway west bound at 2
o'clock in the morning, soaking wet with sweat, but with a
green "passed check-airman" certificate in my pocket. I knew
that tonight had already put me to a level that only a few
ever achieve. Looking back now I see that although it ranked
number one as far as the most exciting night of my life in
airplanes thus far, there were so many, many more to come.

A few days later, I started my first two week tour as First
Officer in a Learjet 24, serial number 142, November triple
seven Mike Romeo (N 777 MR). We flew all over the North
American continent as an Air Ambulance. Our crew always
had a Captain, who was the pilot-in-command, a first officer
who was second-in-command, a nurse, and half the time a
respiratory therapist. Traveling vast distances so very quickly,
life was sure different for me now as compared to when I
was a dairy farmer. After accumulating 800 hours in Learjets
I upgraded to Captain in the fall of 2000. I continued to
fly for Air Response as an air ambulance Captain until I was
put on furlough in the fall of 2001. Soon thereafter I was
hired flying the rich and famous out of the Philadelphia
area and am still doing so today.

The following chapters tell of the everyday occurrences that happened during these flights. The stories come from my journal that I logged faithfully every night. I have tried not to make them any more exciting than what they actually were, keeping them the way they happened, whether good or bad, exciting or boring or normal. As you read this book, I hope you can experience some of the emotions I had while I was living them. I have met and worked with many great people; I have flown some of the world's sleekest jets in the past six years, and looking back right now I feel the same about this as I do about my whole life in general; I wouldn't trade any of it for anything else even if it was possible for me to do so.

None of this new life would have been at all possible for me if it wasn't for the Lady of my life who has always been there supporting me and awaiting my safe return—my dear wife Kathy to whom I dedicate this book.

2. New Professional Pilot Days

Skyhawk 9885 Victor ready for takeoff." I called into the mike. The response came from the tower: "85 Victor, taxi into position and hold runway 18, it will be your next two right hand turns."

"85 Victor," I replied as I smoothly and cautiously began adding just enough power to make this brand new—to me—1976 Cessna roll on the sub-zero ice-cold tarmac at Burlington, Vermont's International Airport. I had just flown up here with Dave Grosbeck and Jeff Noyes in Bob Shirer's Cessna 182 RG, so that I could ferry home Jimmy Longwell's new 180 h.p. Super Skyhawk. Jeff had already left for home in the RG.

Having never flown this particular plane before, and it having a new motor, I am, in my few short minutes on the ground during my run-up trying to know her very intimately before I punch up into the lion's mouth of an approaching winter's storm, which flight service just told me was a mere twenty miles to my south.

As I added this power, my normal and well accustomed world turned chaotic. Adrenalin was just reaching my extremities as I looked through the windscreen only to see the culprit causing all of my inner commotion: A departing F-16 filled my windscreen with at least a ten-foot tail of afterburning fire, shaking and shuddering my airplane, the airport's buildings, and even the ground as I taxied !

As I eased around the second turn to align with runway 19, I couldn't help but notice the Fighting Falcon had already cleared the twelve-mile distant ridge and was but a speck in my window, all of this taking maybe ten seconds worth of time.

"85 Victor, you are cleared for take-off, right hand turn-out approved," said the tower.

"85 Victor cleared for take off," I replied, then added "And don't expect that much performance out of us !"

Tower replied with two clicks of the mike to acknowledge my previous statement as I advanced the throttle to take-off power. As our magic carpet climbed briskly into the frigid Vermont air, I could hardly contain my intense feelings of lust that I have for the greatest occupation on earth—that of a professional pilot !

3. Pre Captain Days

We were wheels up at oh-dark-thirty out of Houston, whose ATIS Whiskey was calling 190, 4,10,15B, 80-OV, 25//24 and 29.97. These abbreviated numbers translate into current flying conditions: Winds from 190 degrees at 4 knots; 10 miles visibility; 1,500 foot broken layer of clouds; 8,000 feet overcast; 25 degrees temperature (Celsius); 24 degrees dew point; and an altimeter setting of 29.97 inches of mercury.

My clearance was to Centennial (APA) via the Hobby 2, Leona transition, direct Rikks, direct APA; 4,000; 390 in 10; squawk 2432. This gave our route of flight to Centennial Field: Climb to 4,000 feet initially; expect 39,000 feet in

10 minutes; in case we loose radio contact on our climb out, dial 2432 into our airplane's transponder which tells air traffic control who we are as well as our airspeed and altitude. No departure frequencies are given when a SID (standard instrument departure) is involved as these are printed onto the charts that we use. These printed charts greatly reduce radio transmission congestion at busy airports.

On our way up to FL390 (flight level of 39,000 feet) I took probably twenty pictures of one of the most picturesque sunrises I've ever seen. I remember telling Tony that some people think these things just happen, but I know there's more to it than that ! The Almighty was really giving us a show. The lights came through the tropical storm's cloud layers in varied colors, which could never be duplicated by man, as we weaved our way heavenward.

Enroute, I pushed the NEAREST button on our smart box and it said we were really close to Winslow, Arizona. Tony flipped on the AM ADF (automatic direction finder) and—by God !— that song was playing by The Eagles: "I'm standing on the corner in Winslow, Arizona, and such a fine sight to see...it's a girl, my Lord, in a flat bed Ford, slowin' down to take a look at me.....", so go figure this one !

Air traffic control said for us to "navigate direct Quail for the Quail 3 arrival, then direct HUNTN' then radar vectors to just outside Casse for the ILS 35Right at APA," and asked if we had the weather.

"Affirm" I said as I rattled back our clearance, and they replied with "expect to cross Quail at 11,000 feet and 250 knots." APA's ATIS Uniform was winds 360 at 6 (from the north at six knots), visibility one mile, 200 foot overcast, light rain and freezing drizzle, mist, temp and dew point both at 6 degrees Celsius, and the altimeter was 29.61— not exactly ideal conditions, if you know what I mean ! We disappeared into the bright white undercast at around 12,000 feet on the altimeter and four intense minutes later at 100 feet above the ground level was one of the best sights you could ever hope to see at such a time...a beautifully lit up runway which we made good use of.

After deplaning and ordering fuel for our next leg to Bellingham, Washington (BLI) I heard at least the next two Jets go missed-approach. We had been fortunate to see the approach lights at the Decision Height of 200 feet above ground level and could continue on down to 100 feet above ground level (AGL) where we had to see one of about eight other items according to the regulation criteria, or else we would have been on our way to Pueblo, Colorado which I had chosen as our alternate.

Out of Denver our clearance was via the Yellowstone 1, Laramie transition, and then as filed: Direct BLI; 8,000; 390 in 10; 132.75 and squawk 0637 in the transponder. When we finally flew far enough northwest bound, about the next five states had received their first snowfall of the year. It was so pretty to see from altitude.

A few miles out, information Victor at BLI reported winds from 020 at 28 knots gusting to 36; 12/03 temp/dew point; and 30.06 on the meter (altimeter). As I descended out of the broken layer about ten miles from our destination, I was surprised when Tony shut down an engine and said to just do a single-engine approach. I sure was surprised if not shocked ! This would be very hard to do in the turbulence, but not impossible. Got her in alright but it wasn't real pretty. Got the job done, but I sure need more practice.

We picked up Karen, our patient, and Doug her husband. They and two other couples had been up here on their vacation when a truck had lost control and flipped over, killing the driver and almost killing the 3 ladies as they were returning from some shopping. Karen had mashed both legs, feet, toes, arms, and had some lacerations, but will eventually heal. Her sister had walked the line between living and not living for hours, but finally life had won this time. She's really badly hurt and can't be moved from the local hospital for months. Their friend was also hurt but not as badly as the other two. The men were playing golf when the accident occurred. We were called and hired to take them both home to Davenport, Iowa (DVN).

We were cleared to our fuel stop in Rapid City, South Dakota, a route straight across the Rockies. We were told to depart runway 34 with a right turn to 100 degrees within 2 miles of the airport, maintain 5,000 and if we could provide our own terrain separation, to climb and maintain 10,000. By this time in the afternoon there were only a few scattered clouds and our course took us directly over the heart of the Cascade Mountains. Washington, Idaho and Montana do truly have some of the most beautiful sights to fly over. They have scenery like no other states.

RAP's "Information Bravo" had winds from 330 degrees at 10 knots, 3 miles of visibility in light rain, snow and mist, 400 foot broken clouds with a 600 foot overcast layer, 3 and 2 on the temperature and dew point spread and 30.01 for an altimeter setting. We shot the ILS to runway 32 and broke out just before minimums into a wet, snowy environment. It was actually cold outside there.

Twenty minutes later we were heading for DVN and for some strange reason were kept at altitude until we were forty miles out; then we were 18,000 feet twenty miles out so we took two vectors to lose altitude and entered a left downwind for runway 15 with the spoilers still up. It was dark and our passengers were glad to be home safe and sound.

As we shut down at the FBO my life long friends, Larry and Helen, were waiting for me so we had a good half-hour talk before heading to our final destination of the day, Detroit's Willow Run airport(YIP). There was a huge thick line of thunderstorms between us and there so we tried to skirt toward the south, heading toward Bloomingdale, Illinois and then on up toward Fort Wayne. But what you see on radar from the ground and what your plane's radar shows in the air may be two different things. As we flew towards Bloomington, many more storms were developing all around us. As Dale Smith, my hired hand on the farm used to say, especially during haying, "It was building."

We were engulfed in lightning for fifteen minutes and 100 miles. I was scared. But the best show of the day was about to begin. Our plane developed St. Elmo's Fire, which is a phenomenon I had read about but had never experienced. Our whole windshield was glowing in a baby blue, zebra striped pattern, and both wingtips were glowing. The electrical charge seemed to stand out or float a good two inches from our surfaces. Scared again! After about five minutes of this show, we broke out into a crisp, clear, black South Chicago sky.

All was well until again in the pattern at Willow Run; good old Tony pulled an engine on me. This time things went much better and we greased down on runway 23 left after working fourteen hours and logging some ten air hours.

This had been one heck of a full day, and the hot shower and king-sized bed had never felt better than they did this night.

The next morning started for me a mere four hours later, when I was allowed to jump seat on a DC 9, with Captain John D.L.C. back to Albany for a week off. John has flown for Northwest for over ten years and I was thrilled to sit up front and help him and his co-pilot Bob. I am going to take my Airline Transport Written Exam around Wednesday, and next Monday I start my upgrade training for Learjet Captain at Flight Safety International in Phoenix.

4. New Captain Days

Well I'm home for a couple of weeks. Probably in a week or so if the dreary winter weather is still with us I'll be telling dispatch to please get me out of this depressing weather the northeast has been plagued with all winter long.

I finished flying this tour with a trip from Chicago MDW (Midway) to Denver's Arapahoe (APA) Centennial airport. Trips into Denver now seem to me like trips going home; there's always a gang to meet us—dispatchers and mechanics—and I'm best friends with all of them.

I jump-seated home to Baltimore's BWI thanks to a Captain Bull D. He welcomed myself and my trusted copilot, A.J., onboard for our free cross-country ride; when it was time to deplane I thanked him again and gave him my card and told him anytime he needed a ride to call my company and maybe we could help as we have an open seat policy for such things also.

While awaiting the departing flight from Denver I was surprised to hear on the PA system: "Captain Dana Van Loan please report to gate 1 !" I jumped out of my seat and as I walked across one of the largest airline terminals in the entire U.S. I couldn't help but show off a dimpled smile with the pearly whites glistening as I thought about where I had been ten years ago, and where I have gone since then in the ensuing ten years !

In 1993 I was still milking cows on our family farm and at the same time trying to squeeze in flying lessons in Ken Kamp's 1966 Cessna 150F at Nellis Field, the little rural airstrip a few miles from our farm; now I'm strutting across this huge international airline terminal in front of hundreds of pairs of eyes in my beautiful new Captain's outfit. I can assure you all that no one loves their job more than I do this one.

This tour was a huge step forward in my airline career as I now have 70 hours under my belt as a Captain and believe me the first few trips were real tough mentally. My friend Raymond Gould told me that it would be tough till I had a hundred or so hours as pilot in command of a jet; for me it seemed to all get really better after about 50 hours. Of course having a great copilot like A.J. helps a lot too ! On the days that we didn't fly I studied the airborne radar books till I was blue in the face. Then I bought another radar book and studied and studied and now I believe I know quite a bit more on this very important subject. But for the next ten days I just need to chill back home with some time off.

5. HALIFAX TO DC TO HOME

We departed Schenectady at 7:00 a.m. and rolled out on a heading of 86 degrees with Halifax, Nova Scotia in our sights. Things were happening quickly. As I climbed through 34,000, I noticed the ground speed was 554 knots, so we leveled off and flew in the jet stream. Fifty-eight minutes later we landed on runway 33 after entering a left base for the visual approach.

Our patient showed up shortly thereafter, a feisty military officer; he was on vacation with his wife and had suffered a stroke, so they needed to return to a hospital near their home, which was in the Washington, DC area. The heading for Washington, DC was west, which seemed surprising to me. The coast of Maine, Cape Cod and Boston looked spectacular from the air. We were flying into worsening weather, and by the time we left the Boston area we were IMC (Instrument Meteorological Conditions), or as we pilots call it "in the soup."

After taking vectors that at the time seemed like going over half of God's creation, we finally intercepted the localizer to runway 01 at Washington National (DCA) and we called the field in sight from three miles out. It was raining very hard and they were very busy. After delivering Reg and Carol to the ambulance, we ordered 180 gallons of jet fuel per side with prist and settled down to get the clearance home.

"November 102 Alpha Romeo is cleared to the Schenectady airport via departing runway 01, noise abatement procedures and P-56 avoidance procedures, radar vectors Smyrna, Victor 271 Swann, Victor 268 Bross, Jet route 42 Robbinsville, direct La Guardia, La Guardia 055 radial to intercept Victor 487 at Trudi, direct Mooni, direct Canan, direct Schenectady, maintain 5,000, expect 290 in ten minutes, departure on 125.65, squawk 5630."

Wow ! This is modern navigation procedures ? In this day and age of precision GPS technology ? It sounds more like "You-sure-can't-get-there-from-here technology !" Anyway, we broke out into VFR conditions around Kingston or so and did the visual into SCH's runway 04. Another very satisfying day filled with airplanes, controllers, and people in need. I am glad that I could help !

6. Mom, Pop, Suzie and Joey

Tuesday started in Denver with a self-audit of my personal pilot file portfolio to make sure everything was current, up-to-date and correct. I had a restless sleep the night before as I was battling a sinus infection with lots of congestion in my head. Kevin Burkhart was teaching a new class of three co-pilots and asked me to sit in if time permitted—as I was on call—and of course I said yes ! We hammered through several differences of systems between the Lear 20s and 30s, a most interesting discussion. Break time one and one-half hours later revealed that Don and I had a possible trip to Montrose, Colorado (MTJ) and on to Palwaukee, Chicago (PWK).

We hustled down to Applebee's for a decent lunch and then headed back to the apartment to change into our uniforms. A short while later we were beeped; sure enough, the money had come through and the trip to Montrose and Chicago was on.

I preflighted November 435JL, a Lear 35, serial #18, while Don ordered the fuel, picked up the trip sheets, etc. Thirty minutes later we launched for MTJ and it was one of the bumpiest twenty-seven minutes of my life. For some reason ATC would not allow us above FL180 so we flew under a bumpy sky full of fair weather cumulus.

When we landed, our new nurse, Scott, went bedside and I ordered fuel, filled our cooler with ice, soda and water, filled the thermos with fresh hot coffee and stocked our little kitchenette with snack food.

It seems our passengers, the Smith's, had flown out west and rented a car to tour the Southwest when they had a car accident, a head-on collision. Mom and Pop were around forty years old; Joey was ten and Susie was twelve. Mom had two black eyes and a few facial lacerations. Joey had a broken left arm, but was all excited about the flight home. Susie fared the worst with a severe cut around the base of her neck and multiple broken bones. She was the one on the stretcher. She had lots of pain. Surprisingly, Pop, the driver, had some bruises but not a scratch.

When the ambulance arrived, all were quite somber except for Joey. In spite of the pain of his broken arm, he was as excited as anyone I had ever seen about the upcoming flight. I could sense this immediately and asked him if he would like to help me load the luggage. His eyes widened and he ran past me and into and through the plane before yelling "You betcha !" He said he was a veteran at flying, said he flew all the time. Said they lived in Chicago near the Palwaukee Airport. Later his dad told me that Joe had flown once locally in Chicago and once commercially to go on this vacation.

The winds at MTJ were from 290 degrees at 11 knots, 10 miles visibility, clear, 35/04, and 30.10 on the altimeter. We taxied out to 35 as it was 2,000 feet longer than the favored runway 31 and we always opt for the longer runway, wind permitting. Twenty-five minutes later we leveled at FL410 after an initial climb of 250 knots to 0.70 Mach. Power was then set at 94 percent fan speed, N1, low pressure side. The temps settled on 780 decrees C, and the fuel meter settled on 600 lbs/side. We had used only 1,200 lbs. on the 25 minute climb to altitude. Impressive numbers to me since I'm a 20-series driver and they are real fuel guzzlers.

This was one of my first ever jaunts in a Lear 35 series jet featuring the turbofan Garrett engines. I recorded after one hour and forty minutes a 2,200 pound total fuel burn, which I would have easily used in the first hour in the Lear 25. In simple terms, this means 40 minutes of free flying with the Lear 35.

ATIS (automatic terminal information service) is the hourly report of current weather conditions at larger airports which is given a different phonetic letter of the alphabet every hour, so when we check in with an approach controller we tell him we have that current weather (in this case, Oscar for the letter "O"). PWK's ATIS Oscar reported winds 290 at 10, and they were using the ILS to 16 (ILS means instrument landing system which is a precision approach giving us both lateral and vertical guidance to usually 200 feet above the ground). Our descent was a 160 mile long zigzag through Chicago's departure air space until we were finally established on the localizer (the extended runway centerline which is our lateral guidance) at 2,600 feet with runway in sight. Vee Ref (landing speed based on weight) at our 13,000 pound landing weight was 119 knots as we chirped three times on a relatively short 5,000 foot-long strip. We do not use finesse on short strips. The name of the game is to get on the mains—get the main landing gears on the ground—and get the jet stopped with braking action as well as with our thrust reversers. There's no being nice to Mr. Goodyear when landing on short strips.

As everyone disembarked, Joey's huge brown eyes were still showing his excitement. He grabbed my right hand and started shaking it and said it had been an awesome flight. Mom and Pop also each shook my hand and thanked me for bringing them safely to home sweet home. Our nurse Scott gave little Susie another pain medication IV and then we loaded her into the ambulance. She was groggy and in a lot of pain, but she tried to smile and looked me in the eyes and said without speaking "Thanks, Dana, for getting me home." I smiled back at her and nodded as if to say "Anytime Susie, anytime. Glad I could help."

7. JIMMY

We had to pick up Jimmy in Pontiac, Michigan. He was twenty-one years young and was about ready to start another semester at his local community college.

But then fate stepped into his path. Jimmy was unloading a flatbed trailer of steel by hand and stacking it on a pile alongside the rig for the Department of Public Works when the pile became lop sided and fell over on him. It snapped his neck.

We airlifted Jimmy and his mom to the renowned Craig institute in my secondary home town of Denver, Co. There he would find the very best care in the world for his type of injury. His mom was very excited that they finally had some new hope that someone, somewhere could help her and her son try to return to a somewhat normal life. Yes, he was paralyzed from the neck down, but maybe, just maybe—she now had new hope as of this flight.

I was feeling okay flying this trip until we had to unload Jim. As I unhooked the aft latch on his stretcher and looked at the sleeping young man, I could not contain the feelings and emotions which suddenly overcame me. I couldn't help but think why in the world this type of tragedy had to happen to such a nice youngster with his whole life ready to blossom into manhood. I thought of my own twenty-one-year-old son back home, Jesse, and how it could have just as well been him, or you, or me. He was just so young. Jimmy was sleeping so he didn't see me, but his mom and every one else saw me silently sobbing as we carried him off of the airplane's stairway. As I helped her into the ambulance after we loaded her son, I gave her a hug and wished them good luck . She hugged me back because she knew how upset I was. She thanked me for the smoothest flight she had ever had.

Then she smiled and said, "Hey, Dana, the doctors have given us new hope, and we're going to start building on our new lives—starting right now, thanks to you guys !"

That seemed to snap me right out of my emotional depression. Today, as in this very instant, was the very beginning of a whole new life for both of them !

8. BAGPIPES AND CUSTOMS

Thursday we left Schenectady for NYC early but, once there, had to wait for medical problems to be resolved, finally departing Teterboro for Sacramento at 4:30 p.m.! Our first fuel stop was in Bloomington, Indiana and the next was to be at Denver––but because there was a tornado near there with hail over one inch in diameter, I said 'maybe next time' and diverted into Scottsbluff, Nebraska. Wow ! The corn was all of six feet tall and a beautiful dark green; that's when I knew I wasn't in upstate New York anymore.

We climbed out between a couple of thunderstorms departing BFF and picked up severe icing and turbulence at the same time. They are no fun. An hour and a half later, just as the sun was setting, we landed at a neat little airport called Lincoln Municipal, which is about thirty miles north of Sacramento in the San Joaquin Valley. On our descent we flew right over Reno and then Lake Tahoe west-bound. That was a long day.

We had brought Jim's eighty-four year old sister Martha home to die. Jim was a really neat Scottish man of seventy-nine years. As I unloaded the baggage his eye twinkled as he pointed to the one thick briefcase. "These are my bagpipes and I can really play them," he said. I asked if I could see them and for the next ten minutes he was rummaging through Scottish outfits and bagpipe pieces. That's what Jim did for fun— he played those pipes. Scottish men are very proud people.

Jim's family ended up giving us a ride about thirty miles away to the Holiday Inn, where I checked in and crashed around midnight—but not before the phone rang from dispatch. We had a trip the following noon back to Rhode Island from San Diego, and Rhode Island meant home to Schenectady after that.

The next day, after flying the length of California on a beautiful Friday morning, we descended just to the west of Los Angeles and into the normal Southern California haze and overcast. We were told to turn left to a heading of 160 degrees, descend and maintain 10,000 feet, and intercept the final approach course for the VOR Alpha approach into San Diego's Brown Field and to report POGIE inbound. Just before arriving at POGIE, center came back with: "102 AR expedite descent **now** to 4,000. Your traffic is an Airbus at your one o'clock and four miles eastbound, climbing out of 8,000."

We were in the smog so I flipped up the boards (spoilers) and descended at 6,000 feet per minute. Those kinds of rides are fun. We usually don't fly like that with paying passengers on board, unless it is absolutely necessary. When you hear the words "expedite" and "now", that's when you do it and don't ask questions.

At POGIE inbound we descended to the 1,260 foot Minimum Descent Altitude and at two miles out called the field in sight.

Tower said "Enter right traffic for 26 right and you are cleared to land number two behind the Cherokee."

So we did. Shortly thereafter our patient arrived from Mexico in a Mexican ambulance. And that's when the trouble began.

I guess the dogs at Customs didn't the like the smell of something inside the ambulance. I believe the two drivers were hauling more things into this country than just our patient, but that's another story in itself. The irate Customs officer told us to get on our way and disappear, which we did. After loading Ralph and his wife, Jeff started to taxi as I got our clearance. "Lifeguard 102 AR is cleared to FOE (Topeka) via the Brown Field IFR departure procedure, radar vectors Julian, direct Parker, direct Drake and then as filed. Climb and maintain 3,000. Expect 410 in 10 minutes. Contact departure control on 125.15 and squawk 7363."

A while later we saw Phoenix slip by on the right followed by the famous meteor crater site, which was made by a meteor the size of a building traveling at the speed of sound; the crater must be about a mile across. After that we flew over Winslow, Arizona, probably named after my dog. That's about it. We fueled in Topeka and landed in Providence after shooting the ILS 23. We did coast-to-coast in just five hours to the minute. As soon as we touched down, Ralph's wife yelled: "Ralph, we're home !" Unfortunately, Ralph, too, had come home to spend his last few days.

After buying 200 gallons per side of fuel and flying through a line of thunderstorms twenty-five miles thick,

Albany and Schenectady appeared in the window and the rest is history.

Home again and, once again, feeling pretty good about myself, helping other people and their families. I can't save Jim's sister, or Ralph, but by God I sure did help them out the best I could.

9. Lake Effect Snow

I met one of the nicest fellows the other day as I loaded him into our Learjet for a flight from Nashville's BNA airport to Syracuse, New York's SYR. Brian had bone cancer and had just received his second bone marrow transplant done within the past two years, at Nashville; now he was returning home. Actually, his home was in a town southwest of Syracuse called Keuka Park. He was in excruciating pain and was relocating to a Syracuse hospital to be nearer his home in case he ever became well enough to actually go back home, which was doubtful. His wonderfully optimistic wife, Kathy, rode in the jet near him; our crew consisted of nurse Scott Walker Useman, first officer A.J. Catone, and myself.

The weather had been great during our two-day layover in Nashville but would change as we ventured northward. The only snow in the nation on this particular day was a heavy band of lake effect stuff from Buffalo to Utica, including of course our preferred destination SYR, Syracuse, and alternate, ROC, Rochester, NY. I kept my eye on the WSI weather computers at Mercury Air Center as Scott was picking up our patient.

It was an afternoon flight with a proposed 2 p.m. wheels-up time. We had arrived at 12:30 p.m. to get ready. Usually the ambulance picks up our nurse at the airport and that's when I like to show up for work also. Most of the time there's also a thirty-minute ride both to and from the hospital and a forty-minute prep time while at the hospital. Of course these usual numbers vary greatly depending on city, time of day, and so on. Things happen much faster at Bismark, South Dakota at midnight than they do in downtown Philadelphia on a Monday morning—you get the picture.

At any rate, Walker usually calls me when he is 20 minutes out and that's when we pilots start really getting ready, doing all of the last minute details and such. Syracuse's weather was varying each half-hour with ceilings pretty much stabilized at 300 feet but visibilities were ranging from a half mile to one mile in snow and mist. I would check ROC's and UCA's weather each time a new forecast came in and pretty much it was useless to try and get a feel for a trend. There was no trend for the weather on this trip. As Forest Gump would say, the weather at our destination would be like a box of chocolates—you never know what you're going to get till you get there !

So my simple plan was to get there, and if we couldn't get in, we would go to the closest alternate that we could get into. ROCs' and UCA's as well as SYR's had been fluxuating all day long, but in a worst case scenario we could always go to Albany if the whole plan went south, as we had plenty of fuel.

For those of you that don't fly too much— lake effect snow is almost as much a hazard as ground fog; you can't really do much to beat it since you cannot see through it. Pretty much it means "time for plan B," your alternate.

We left BNA on time and with the help of a nice 80 knot quartering southwest tail wind we found ourselves 120 miles out of SYR about an hour later asking for lower. It was now time to work. I asked A.J. to get SYR's weather again—as he had at 200 miles out—as well as our three nearest alternate airports' weather. The time to divert would have been now, before we plunged down into the lousy winter weather. SYR was now down to three-quarters of a mile visibility as we started our vector to Stoda intersection in preparation for the ILS to runway 28. The ride was not too pleasant with turbulence and lots of icing, but I'm sure the passengers didn't notice. Lears can fly in almost any weather compared to most planes.

The level of concentration beginning an approach to minimums is intense. A.J. and I work very well together, and we both really enjoy the challenges in doing these approaches. Now I flew one of the best approaches of my career and at the middle marker, which was a half-mile out from the threshold, A.J. called the runway in sight and the rest was history.

We unloaded our man and his wife into the waiting ambulance on the Executive Aviation ramp, wishing them the best of luck. Brian had served two tours in Viet Nam and his suffering was due to him being exposed to a chemical known as Agent Orange. I felt so badly for him and can only hope and pray that he doesn't need to suffer too much more. They both thanked me for the awesome flight, as they both loved to fly, and this one they said had been one of their best. After the ambulance had left the gate, I quickly filed our next flight plan to Schenectady, and twenty-four minutes later I was done with yet another very satisfying and rewarding day.

Good luck Brian !

10. DOROTHY, PHIL AND THE DOGS

Phil was a sweetheart of an 83 year-old man. Dorothy, his wife, was also a very pleasant lady. Also onboard were their two Chihuahuas named Tasmanian Devil and Tequila. The two dogs were not quite so accommodating as were their masters.

I learned while loading Phil that he had worked as an engineer on various aircraft brake systems throughout his career, including the systems on the big Boeing 747s, 737s, the space shuttles and even the B1B bombers. Although he labored intensively just trying to speak, his eyes told his story the best.

We picked this family up at Fox Field in Lancaster, California near Los Angeles. Phil had had an accident unloading his tow vehicle from behind his R.V. and was basically knocked down and run over by his own truck as it coasted off its base. His shoulder had been injured and he also had some lacerations. Being an elderly diabetic didn't help at all, so the bad situation seemed to only get worse. Bedsores and kidney problems forced Phil to give up his traveling in his golden years and we took him safely back home to Panama City, Fla. where I believe he'll remain for the rest of his days.

I can just imagine how proud he must feel every time he sees an airplane which uses a braking system which he helped design. I could tell he was a proud man and I bet he lived a proud life. And I was one very proud pilot myself being given the opportunity to serve and help him out at a time when he really needed help. So thanks, Phil, for sharing a few moments of your story with me. I know you could not speak any more than you did but your eyes and expressions said it all . And thank you Lord, for letting me help Phil, Dorothy, and—even Tequila and the Tasmanian Devil.

11. Into Las Vegas

The beeper sounded at 11:30 and by 1:30 I and my Denver-based crew were ready for take-off when the tower asked me to call them on the land line. They asked if our flight to Las Vegas was time-critical as the weather at McCarran was real poor and planes were not able to arrive due to low clouds and poor visibilities resulting from fog and rain of nearby thunderstorms.

"I guess we can wait a while for the weather to change," I told them, and waited another hour as I watched the special reports come out of Tac-Air's weather computer on the Centennial ramp.

About every twenty minutes I was reading new weather conditions and sure enough, in seventy-five minutes it looked better, so fifteen minutes later I was screaming down Centennial's runway 17 Left on the Denver 3 Standard

Instrument Departure with radar vectors to intercept the
Denver 220 degree radial to the 80 DME (mile) fix, then
direct Blue Mesa VOR direct Nootn for the Fig Nootn Three
Arrival into Las Vegas' McCarran International Airport
(LAS). Maybe twenty minutes later our clearance was
amended to direct Phigg, expect to cross Phigg at 11,000
feet with no speed restrictions. An hour later as we
approached that intersection, we were given vectors for the
ILS 25 Left approach, immediately followed with a speed
restriction to maintain 170 knots. We were still indicating
all of 250 knots so up came the spoilers and back came the
trimming button and maybe twenty seconds later we were
on a new heading awaiting localizer intercept at 170 knots
with the boards (spoilers) again put away and 10 degrees of
approach flaps set. As the localizer came alive, approach told
us to track inbound and to maintain 200 knots until we
were on a ten mile final, and that we were cleared for the
approach and, if able, to sidestep to runway 25 Right, and
also to be cautious for wake turbulence as we were in a four-
mile trail of a 757 on this same approach.

My trusted co-pilot Bill Lundin was handling all of the
radios and helping me immensely, calling out distances,
speeds and altitudes. Teamwork ! The weather was very
turbulent, lots of icing in the overcast and then lots of rain
as we descended from our interception altitude of 8,000
feet down the slide to our decision height of 2,317 feet which
put us 250 feet above the runway. I remember telling Bill
that I was going to fly the glide slope one dot high for
avoidance of the 757's wingtip vortices and at the ten-mile
fix I called for flaps 20, gear down, landing checks, please,
as I wanted to stay as far from the big Boeing as I could
safely do, which meant to fly as slow as I was capable of
flying.

Finally, at the eight-mile fix, which was just outside the final approach fix, I called for full flaps, saw my blue light outer marker indicator flash as well as hearing the audible tones from the marker, and as the glide slope was still at the one dot high position, I reduced the power about five percent and watched the Instantaneous Vertical Speed Indicator settle on 700 feet per minute as the great white jet was finally all configured to land and was doing everything I had asked of it. Bill was still performing his duties flawlessly, and at about 500 feet above decision height we broke out of the clouds and there were the twin runways . Bill called our sidestep and we were cleared to land on the right, and soon thereafter the tower controller thanked us for all of our fine work. "Anytime" we answered, as we greased N700FC onto the tarmac.

12. Leaving Las Vegas

The two nurses went to the Las Vegas hospital as Bill and I got to work. We needed to take a top ex-Iranian General to Nashville, Tennessee, as he was very ill. I loaded the plane with 925 gallons of jet fuel and rechecked the weather, then filed two amended flight plans to Nashville's BNA with a fuel stop in Wichita's ICT. airport. I didn't like the forecast and current weather at ICT and felt more comfortable with a fuel stop in SLN (Salina, Kansas) as their weather was supposed to stay above a 200 foot ceiling and visibilities were to stay greater than a half mile for our arrival time at 9 p.m., as it was now 6 pm. I changed the first destination to SLN and the next departure from there also at 9:30 and filed LIT (Little Rock, Arkansas) as our alternate as SLN was not supposed to be all that good; we were required by regulation to file an alternate and LIT was to remain in VFR (visual flight rules) all evening as the Midwestern low pressure area moved ever so slowly eastward. I called dispatch and told them of my plan; they took care of calling our old and new destinations to cancel, and also ordered our catering as well as coordinated fueling and fire truck necessities. Whenever we refuel with patients onboard we need to have a fire truck and firemen standing by.

Finally with all of the forthcoming trip's details set to my liking, I received a beep from headquarters and called them right back only to find our general had become too sick to move and that we should stay there overnight and see how he was the next morning.

OK…time for plan B. I asked my trusted copilot Bill to try and find some reasonable rooms for the night, that we needed four of them, and as usual, try to get them at a really nice place without spending very much money, and man did we strike gold ! The famous gold pyramid-shaped Luxor offered us four rooms at a great price which was around sixty-nine dollars per day, so when our two nurses Julia and Patty returned, off we all went for a very special evening spent in one of the coolest, most exotic hotels this old country boy had ever seen ! Huge statues of Egyptian sphinxes and Pharaohs and Empresses everywhere ! We enjoyed a terrific Mexican dinner and later a walk on the strip followed by watching people gambling away wads of money in the casinos. I slept very well.

The next morning I was up at 6 o'clock and checked the weather immediately to find out if this trip would be a go. If the trip was on, I needed to find another place for fuel as the whole central U.S. was having an ice storm and if I could help it I would avoid it. I came up with a plan for a one hour hop over to Albuquerque (ABQ) New Mexico, for fuel, and then a two-and-a-half-hour leg over all of the bad weather in the Midwest to our destination BNA. At 8 o'clock Julia, the head nurse, called my room and said the patient was better and the trip was a go. I called the others and we all met in the lobby at 9 o'clock. We were airborne by 10:20, following the Oveto Three departure procedure with the Dove Creek transition to ABQ with six onboard...Bill & I up front, Julia and Patty our two nurses, the General on the stretcher and the General's wife on the back divan. Our arrival was direct Curly from Dove Creek for the Curly 2 arrival; forty minutes later were airborne on the ABQ 1 departure procedure which is simply vectors for obstacle clearance and before we knew it we were cleared direct Graham for the Graham Four Arrival and to cross Graham at 10,000 feet and 250 knots. Soon I was greasing the Learjet onto runway 02 left, contacting the tarmac at about 118 knots of indicated airspeed.

The ambulance was awaiting the general and his wife and they were home safe and sound four hours after we had departed LAS. As for myself and my crew, we now had to explore Nashville !

Chapter 13. FINALLY TO ALASKA

The beeper sounded shortly after landing at Denver. We had done another Craig trip from Detroit to Centennial Airport and were ready to start relaxing. Craig trips always involve either paraplegics or quadriplegics as this sort of rehabilitation is what the Craig people specialize in. I called the office and they said I had a Phoenix-to-Calgary trip tomorrow morning with a possible Alaska trip after that. I was excited with a capital E! I had not yet done our 49th state, and I wanted this trip badly.

The next morning finally came and after an hour of flight planning, aircraft stocking, and refueling, we blasted down Centennial's runway 17 Left on our hour-and-twenty-minute flight to Phoenix's Sky Harbor airport. Here we picked up a nice Canadian lady, Betty, who had only been in PHX a week when she suffered a stroke. She was a Canadian citizen who wintered in the warm land and summered in her hometown of Calgary. Her recovery was doing fine and, as usual, the Canadian nationalized insurance people paid us to bring her home for her recovery. Her husband owned a huge auto dealership and had flown down commercially to accompany his ailing wife back to the north country.

The trip to Calgary was one of the most beautiful I have ever been privileged to fly. Leveling off at our initial cruising altitude of FL370 (flight level of 37,000 feet), I looked down on the Navajo Nation, the Grandest of Canyons, Lakes Powell and Mead, Page with her tall smokestacks and the Glen Canyon National Park. My camera was very busy, and I even narrated as a tour host to Bob and Betty. They loved this trip and vowed to never again fly commercially with the major airlines.

We passed the Great Salt Lake and then were awed as the rugged Sawtooth and Bitteroot mountain ranges of Idaho silently slipped by. Soon we were watching Montana's Rockies, then Butte and the capital, Helena, slide on by our right wing as well, but the weather was rapidly deteriorating in front of us. Before long we were on our 130 mile descent into a cold and snowy Alberta and sure enough the ATIS was calling visibility of two miles and a ceiling of 800 feet in blowing snow. Soon we were on the localizer and a few minutes later were parked alongside our awaiting ambulance with more excited family members, ending yet another fine and satisfying day, for me, helping my fellow man—and having enjoyed such fascinating views from my front office.

The next morning we found several inches of fresh Canadian snow so I called the FBO and had them hangar the plane as dispatch thought the Anchorage trip might sell and if it did we could relocate there maybe later in the afternoon. I told them it would be nice to see this trip in the daylight hours rather than at night; and, God, I had waited my whole life to see Alaska and now I might just get to see some of her sights ! Then the beeper sounded again, and a quick enthusiastic call to Darren at dispatch revealed that the trip was sold and we could go as soon as we wanted. Wow ! Great ! Alaska ! In the daylight !

An hour later we were level at 39,000 feet watching the most mountainous, most rugged terrain in this world slip by. I remember thinking out loud to Scott, my nurse, that this old world is not crowded, that there's lots and lots of space left for people to live, at least that's how it looked from this perspective. We finally saw a town below after an hour of nothing but mountains and it was a four corners called Prince George, where Canada's Yellowhead Highway, Cariboo Highway and John Hart Highway cross in the wilderness. The next town was Prince Rupert and then Juneau nestled near lots of icy water. The Coastal Mountain Ranges I cannot describe—they have to be seen and experienced, words do them no justice. My camera was busy again.

The next hour was flown above an undercast with occasionally only a mountain top showing through, and soon we were on our descent, an exciting descent for me. I was tingling all over with emotions knowing my next landing was going to be in the state I had wanted to visit since early childhood. As we descended through the layers of clouds, the turbulence was moderate and occasionally more than that, as I slowed to point seven three Mach for our turbulent air penetration speed, and then to 250 knots as the mach meter disappeared at 29,000 feet giving way to the indicated airspeed in knots. And then I saw lights, and water, and a city, and a river, and a bay, and then an ocean too.

It was getting near dusk and the sun was very low. But there was my city ! My destination ! My lifelong dream land––and then it was gone. Some weather was moving in from the Bering Sea and I needed the localizer to finish my task. We were given a choice for runways, and I told them the ILS for runway 19 would be just fine and before you knew it we broke out of the clouds and greased the great magic carpet onto Alaskan soil. It was a very exciting landing and taxi for me; we had the boys put our plane in a warm hanger and then we were off for a day exploring Anchorage as our trip started the next night at 8 p.m. and was to Atlanta, Georgia.

The TV crews were at the Anchorage airport the next night. Our patient was well known and certainly well liked by all. Rick was a newspaper publisher. Rick had taken an afternoon off from work a couple of days before and had taken a walk with his dog, Boozer, a chocolate Labrador. It was raining at the office in downtown Anchorage, but Rick knew the mountains were getting snow, so he and Boozer drove up the road to the Glenn Alps parking lot and then started hiking up the Flat Top trail he and his chocolate Lab pal had hiked so many times before. Rick was an experienced mountaineer, you see, and when he reached the fork where the new trail splits from the old, they went left onto the old trail, around Blueberry Hill, to the point where the old trail turns and goes virtually straight up 1,000 feet to Flattop's summit. As Rick kicked each step through the snow for solid footing, all of a sudden the whole gully released, and a heartbeat later Rick and Boozer were hurling downhill, out of control, ass-over-tea-kettle, caught in an avalanche ! Then, as fast as it had happened, it was over, there was nothing moving and all was very quiet. Rick thought he was half buried in the snow, as he could not move, but then he saw his legs and said, I'm not buried, I'm paralyzed !

Help me, help me, he cried out over and over again to no one in particular. Then the pain hit him; his back, his face, his teeth, and his lungs felt like a freight train had ran over him. And then, miraculously, two words ran through the blackness of his agony— CELL PHONE ! Rick had kept it in his backpack's top pocket but had no idea where it had ended after his 600 foot descent. He looked around and amazingly there it was, about six feet away from him! He crawled on his belly and grabbed the phone from the zippered pocket. He then thought of Boozer and started yelling for him. Boozer lay thirty feet away with his left hind leg partially ripped off but soon he came crawling up to Rick; man and best friend lay together in the snow, both slowly bleeding to death. Rick had smashed his mouth and teeth and was bleeding badly from other head wounds. He had several shattered ribs which had punctured both lungs, a severed spinal chord, and a broken back. Several frostbitten fingers were soon to follow on his injury list but he was alive and determined to live ! Then—his phone rang and it was his girlfriend calling to see if everything was all right. He told her where he was and that he was badly hurt, was apparently paralyzed, and in need of a helicopter ambulance. He told her again his location, and that he loved her, and for her to go to the hospital and wait for him there, and then he hung up.

Thirty minutes later a helicopter showed up and found Rick's position, but couldn't land as the winds had picked up to near gale force strength; also, the terrain was so steep they couldn't land, so they called in another chopper with an emergency crew and an air-lift hoist. By the time they arrived and the first paramedic was holding Rick, his fingers were frostbitten and his body temperature had fallen to 85 degrees. He lay head down on a 35 degree slope and, although uncomfortable, the position probably increased the blood flow to his brain and helped him to remain conscious and to avoid brain damage.

Both Rick and Boozer were air-lifted and taken to the hospital where help was waiting. To warm up his body temperature doctors pumped hot water into every body orifice and they say that's when Rick became very vocal. Soon the neurosurgeons removed bone fragments and splinters from Rick's spinal chord and installed titanium rods to stabilize his fractured vertebrae. Boozer was taken to his vet and is well on the road to recovery.

As I said, when Rick arrived at the Anchorage airport for the flight to Atlanta, the press and TV people were all there wishing him the best of luck in his future. We were taking him to the Shepherd Facility which specializes in rehabilitation for such spinal chord injuries. The weather was lousy as an ice storm was about ready to change the runway conditions at Anchorage but we managed to depart just prior to the deteriorating conditions. Rick was accompanied by his girl friend and his best guy friend as we blasted off around 9 p.m. I stopped at 3 a.m. in Billings, Montana, after a four hour flight in the Canadian darkness. As we departed Billings a major winter storm was approaching and again, we snuck out just ahead of it; three hours later Rick was in Atlanta on his way to the Shepherd Center in a ground ambulance.

This was to be the first day for Rick of a new life. He told me as we loaded him into the ambulance that he was lucky as heck to be alive, and that he was going to prove the doctors wrong as they said it was doubtful he would ever walk again. After all, he said, it was unlikely he would survive such an avalanche and fall as he did, and it was just as unlikely he would take such a fall to begin with.

"I'm lucky as hell, really," he said. "To think I'm alive when I should be dead !"

My hat comes off to you, Rick, as you have shown me courage that few possess, and you will remain in my thoughts and prayers. I'm glad I met you and could help you out my friend !

14. Winter Concerns

Today was full of challenges. First off, our runway was white with maybe a half to an inch of packed snow. Out came the big thick Pilot Operating Handbook for the specialty charts that we hardly use every day, since we have abbreviated checklists for the more normal flying conditions.

OK, after I ran the numbers, I needed to multiply my BFL (balanced field length) of 3,000 by 1.7 for a total BFL of 5,100, which left us 300 feet to spare. That means we have enough available runway for departing as 40N has 5,400 feet of tarmac. Hmm; since our runway also slopes downhill about a percent and a half, I lowered our Vee1 take-off decision speed from 122 to 100 knots to give me some margin should something go awry. My briefing to 'the Man' (Charlie Dog, my trusty copilot) was simple: "I am not going to abort for anything after I see 100 knots and if we do have a problem we'll dump fuel and fly to Wilmington, Delaware, or to Philly, depending on the problem. ILG is 7,000 feet and PHL over 10,000 feet long, and if we need to land immediately after take off, I will reverse the departure path and land back here (oh my God) uphill on runway 11."

The Garrets developed their power early in the roll and acceleration is spirited this time of year to say the least. With any load less than 3/4 of fuel, I have to be easy adding thrust or else all the charts, maps, cookies, newspapers, coats, hats and thermoses full of coffee will end up on the back seat on our clients laps ! Last summer 95 percent Fan Speed (N -1) was needed for take-off power as compared to 93 percent with our below freezing temps we have now. For you piston drivers, take-off thrust with my 16,000 pound Lear 35A equals around 17,500 horsepower equivalent so if you reduce these values evenly you will see that this would mean your 160 horse Skyhawk would get up and go with over a 2,000 horse power engine... and when I left Trenton this noon, I weighed only 12,000 pounds and still took off with 17,500 h.p., equivalent to a Hawk climbing with a 3,500 horsepower engine...you get my point.

Anyway, we flew to Wilmington, North Carolina with 150 knots of wind on the nose. That's bad but we were lucky today as the second leg after we picked up our British friend would be back north to Trenton with the same winds—as in horrendous tail winds !

Washington Center had their moments with us today, you never know what kind of a day you're about to have down around here until it has already happened. I do recall being 'step climbed' a thousand feet at a time from home until I saw Norfolk at the 10 o'clock position on my radar return and I also remember having 'the Man' request our cruise-filed altitude of 39,000 feet with two different sectors only to hear, "Sorry, 310 will be your final today." (in the bowels of that jet stream).

Leaving Wilmington, N.C. is always a blast; clearance is always climb to 10,000 feet on course, and checking in with Center at around 10 is when they started in with us again: Turn left 30 degrees followed with numerous level offs and heading changes. Finally I was told to fly direct to Nottingham and to join the Dupont 4 arrival from there. Shortly after passing OTT, we were again given vectors to the west and also started descending already from 310 down into the twenties, and were again told to fly this time direct Jaybo and to cross it at 15,000 feet.

A few minutes later the next sector guy yelled at me and said I was north of our course, to which I told Charlie to tell him we had been on a vector and that we were correcting. A minute later the sector guy said in an irritated voice, "200 Tango Whiskey you are very uncooperative today, turn 90 degrees right and rejoin the arrival !"

I could feel my blood pressure sky rocket with such shenanigans that we had been put through by Center on this day. Never before was I so happy as when we were finally told and did check in with Philly Approach, followed by a nice visual arrival and landing at Trenton, Mercer County, New Jersey. Our British CEO was extremely happy that we had arrived early as our departure time had been 11:01 a.m., which was one minute behind schedule. I remember thanking him for flying with us, and told him that we had probably flown an extra hundred miles with today's routings !

I called Chester County for a runway condition report as Charlie walked our passenger to his awaiting Limo. Bill at dispatch said there was no change from this morning. I had purposely taken minimum fuel leaving ILM as I wanted to land home as light in weight as I could safely be so that in my final approach my speed would be as low as possible, because our landing speed (V ref) is a speed based on weight, and we would be landing with 1,200 pounds of fuel making our plane's weight 11,200 pounds—making V-ref 112 knots which is a lot nicer than 120 knots or so. Ten knots less of touchdown speed makes a huge difference on the roll-out distance.

At any rate I flew the plane landing on the first foot or so of runway, held the nose high for aerodynamic braking as I firmly used the toe brakes, and we slowed to taxiing speed in half of the 5,400 available feet. Once I knew we had it made, I pushed hard on the brakes while slowing on the hard packed snow to find the anti-skid system working superbly. Just before a skid can develop the brakes will release, then brake, then release and so on. The other cold winter weather 'trick' I used for all three approaches today was to cycle the brakes when we would lower the gear for landing: Gear down and locked, turn the anti-skid off, pump the brakes 10 times very aggressively, turn back on the anti-skid, and land normally. This assures the brakes are not frozen from departing in slush, snow and water and then flying along at altitude in 70 degrees below zero air. The other trick that helps is to not retract the gear as fast as usual after rotation. I left it down until our speed approached 200 knots, and this extra 'blow dryer' effect helps to clear the snow and slush from the landing gear extremities also. Another day in the logbooks and a couple more dollars well earned.

15. FLIGHT PLANNING THOUGHTS

It's time to flight plan the 40 N to Jackson Hole (JAC), and back to 40 N for Wednesday's trip. I need to leave JAC at 11a.m. Mountain Daylight Savings Time, or for the elimination of confusion, at 17 Zulu time––Universal Time Coordinated (UTC), or Greenwich Mean Time (GMT), however you prefer to say it. Since the new time changes as of this morning at 2:30 a.m. or so, the way I figure Zulu (from my home base in the Eastern Time Zone) is that noon time is 16 Zulu, and 8 p.m. or 2000 local is 0000Z, simple enough ? Zulu days actually start at 8 pm on the previous day !

Flight planning considerations for the trip to JAC from 40 N are many: Having enough runway to take off considering our weight, the temperature on Wednesday morning, the fuel burn enroute so as to figure landing there or at the alternate landing site with at least the minimum

IFR (instrument flight rules) reserves required by law, and by me of 45 minutes, which I always call 1,200 pounds if it is VFR (visual flight rules).

The trip is 1,565 nautical miles, not even counting flying east after departure as Philly requires us do; then we fly north for a stretch, then finally westbound after reaching Pottstown which must be 25 miles north of here. All told, departing Coatesville westbound adds an extra 40 nautical miles to the totals, as we need to first fly east and then north. Such is the price paid in busy airspace.

The total distance to JAC thereby becomes over 1,600 nautical miles. In a no-wind scenario this would take me around 4 hours to fly. My Lear 35A, N200TW that I'll be flying is a 4-hour machine, landing with an hour's worth of reserve fuel. I could maybe go non-stop with no head winds, but this will not happen on Wednesday. With an average 50 knots of head wind we add an extra half hour to the trip, and with 75 knots of wind on the nose we'll add an additional forty-five minutes.

There, we've already figured that we need a fuel stop enroute. One of the nice features of the 36A that I used to fly was that it held an additional hour's worth of fuel and could routinely fly coast to coast non-stop, that is, if I had a runway that was long enough at my departure airport. Also, the beauty of dead-heading (flying without passengers) to JAC is that I can stop anywhere I'd like for fuel and where the weather also suits my fancy. Choices are practically anywhere in Iowa or Nebraska or southern Minnesota, or even South Dakota. Sioux Falls has a great airport with great approaches and a good fuel price too. I'll be leaning towards a stop at Sioux Falls for sure if the weather is decent there.

From 40 N to FSD is 1,000 miles and three hours; that means 5,500 pounds of fuel required on board when leaving home. After a twenty-minute quick turn there for refueling, we'll have another 1.5 hours to get to Jackson Hole.

Leaving the Hole also requires much thought. I will probably need to leave with 5,600 pounds of fuel as I'll probably burn 4,400 pounds in the 3.5 hour non-stop flight back home. My two passengers and their luggage will total 500 pounds leaving me with a gross take off weight of 16,000 pounds. The Jackson Hole Airport sits at an elevation of 6,500 feet above sea level and only has a length of 6,300 feet. Runway required for my 16,000 pound aircraft if the temperature is 50 degrees will be 5,900 feet, but if its 60 degrees, balanced field length will scoot up to 6,450 feet. That requirement is more than what I have available, so if its 58 degrees or warmer I cannot leave there with enough fuel for a non-stop flight to 40N. Of course, the cooler the better for airplane performance, so if its 40 degrees we'll only need 5,200 feet for our balanced field length.

I'll try to catch the temperature forecasts a day ahead to get an idea of what to expect. I'm betting on 50 degrees at 11a.m. local departure time. Of course, if the weather is down at all back home at Coatesville I would want some extra fuel for the approach and (also for holding reserves) figured into my total, so as you can see there are many variables involved and not much leeway when departing from a high and short airport on a 1,600 nautical mile trip in a Lear 35. Thus a fuel stop on the way back home certainly makes a lot of sense. Fuel at JAC is a lot more expensive than fuel at Sioux Falls too. This can easily add up to a $400 savings !

16. CRITICAL MIDNIGHT RUNS

At my home in upstate New York, I had turned my bedroom lights out at 11 p.m. At 12:45 a.m. some lady in Chicago died in a car accident. Also, at the same time, somewhere in Vermont a 34 year- old lady waited desperately for two kidneys, a pancreas, and a liver. Somehow in the next fifteen minutes these last two scenarios were matched and I received the call at exactly 1:00 a.m. "Sure, I'm on my way in five minutes," was my groggy reply to Brent, our nighttime dispatcher.

After a coffee and a weather briefing while driving my car to the airport, Jeff and I blasted our way out of home base Schenectady (SCH) for Burlington, Vermont (BTV). There were several thunderstorms between us and Burlington, so we navigated towards Saranac Lake until we were past the storms and then were recleared direct to BTV.

Radar really wasn't necessary for storm avoidance; because of the brilliant flashes of lightning we could see each storm cell clearly.

Burlington's tower was closed at this time of night so we took vectors from Boston Center for the ILS 15. Piece of cake. We let her roll long and exited at the end to Valet Air's charter hanger where we met the fuel guy, and also our awaiting patient, her husband, her sister and her brother-in-law. After a quick top-off of fuel into the wings, tips and 1,000 pounds in the trunk, I filed the next leg to Chicago on 122.6, which is the frequency for the on-field Flight Service Station called Burlington Radio. The line guy charged us $95.00 just to come in and pump the fuel after hours; oh well, can't say that I blame him. He had probably worked the whole previous day there anyway.

The race was on. A liver is only good for five or so hours, and the ambulance ride from Chicago's airstrip to the operating table would be 30 minutes. Jeff fired up the left side and started the pre-taxi checks as I received clearance from Boston through 122.6. Burlington Radio responded in a minute after talking on the land line and said,"Lifeguard 102 Alpha Romeo (our Lear 25) is cleared to Chicago's Midway airport as filed,125.27, squawk 7103, climb to and maintain flight level 410.

An unrestrained climb on course to 41,000 feet is pure music to our ears at such a crunch time ! After engine number 2 was on line, and after a current limiter check, we accelerated down runway 33 using 4,000 feet to achieve V1, which was 135 knots indicated airspeed. Vr (rotation) was 136 knots, and V2 (climb out speed) was 135. At V1 we have to fly no matter what happens, its otherwise known as take-off decision speed. At Vr we rotate and fly, and if we lose an engine or anything else we must maintain at least the V2 speed of 135 knots in order to meet the positive climb gradient and to have sufficient directional control in case we lose an engine. At positive rate, I called gear up, and a second later called yaw damper on. In another four seconds I called V ref plus 30, flaps up and, after take-off, checklist please.

Jeff continued on the checks as I settled down in my seat and immersed myself into the ship's soul—climb at 98 percent N2 at 250 knots to 10,000 feet, then trim her down about four nudges with the right thumb to achieve 300 kias; and on modified Mark II wings we can go right up to 370 kias (knots of indicated airspeed) to around 29,000 feet where indicated airspeed in knots gives way to the Mach meter, and then climb at Mach 0.73 or so and hopefully we'd see 2,000 feet per minute to 390, where again only a thumb's touch is needed, nosing down somewhat to 700 fpm until leveling at flight level 410.

Just a quick note here that altitudes from sea level through 17,999 feet are spoken in thousands of feet. From 18,000 to however high you can fly is reported in flight levels, so 19,000 feet would be flight level one-niner zero and 17,000 feet is called one-seven-thousand feet. The lowest flight level is one-eight-zero. I think we were level and accelerating to 0.82 Mach in 20 minutes and 1,300 pounds of fuel since departing BTV.

The night skies were charming, and we flew in "continuous light chop" from around Rochester to near Cleveland, where finally we again found smooth air. Again, the time of day (less traffic) aided our flight and we were told by Chicago Center to descend and maintain 11,000. At around 110 miles out I reduced thrust to 88 percent and trimmed nose down for Mach 0.78 then trimmed again for 1,500 fpm descent initially. Set the cabin to field elevation of 630 feet and as the air thickened, increased rate to 2,000, then 2,500, then 3,000 fpm for rate of descent. If you start to get behind, less power and more nose down—whatever it takes.

We intercepted the ILS 31 center and tracked it inbound to 4,000 feet msl where we sidestepped to the right 90 degrees and entered a high left base for 22 Left. Being slightly higher than I wanted, I called for gear down as soon as I slowed to 200 kias. Once we had three green and no reds on the landing gear indicator and 200 knots, I called for flaps 20 degrees and landing checks please.

As the visual glideslope became red over white, I called flaps 40 and powered up to 83 percent. Piece of cake. Greased her on again.

The ambulance was just pulling onto our ramp and we shut down together. After everyone was together inside the front door of the FBO, we all got together in silence and prayed for our patient, Kerry. We prayed together in silence holding hands, and then Jeff and I walked all four of our passengers to the ambulance. With teary eyes, they all shook our hands, patted our backs, and thanked us from the bottoms of their hearts for making a difference in their lives.

With God's Will, Kerry should be in the recovery room right now.

17. ROOMY AIRPORTS

I was catching up on some rest and relaxation in Atlanta, Georgia in a real nice hotel called the Wingate when the beeper sounded. Dispatch had a trip for us to Chicago's O'Hare Airport (ORD), then to Colorado Spring's Mountain City Airport (COS) and then back home to Denver's Centennial Airport, our home base (APA).

It seems a 25 year-old fellow had fallen down a steep mountain side while hiking in Switzerland on vacation with his friends and had fractured a couple of vertebrae in his back. His father was a physician in Colorado Springs; he had hired a nurse from abroad and nine rear seats of a Swiss Air 747 to bring Randy to ORD; there we would pick him up and finish the transport to COS in our cozy Lear 35.

Everything went smoothly on this second Friday in August. The air aloft was unusually smooth and there were no clouds from PDK in Atlanta until we crossed the

Colorado border where there were a few big scattered thunderstorms. However with our colored radar it was sort of easy flying around and in between the cells.

After a vector taking us away from the airport, I was headed inbound to COS at a thirty-degree angle to intercept the localizer to 35 Left. When finally established, ATC called me and reported a thunderstorm in progress on the field right where we wanted to go, with lots of lightning and turbulence. They suggested a sidestep to 35 Right if and when we went into visual conditions.

So be my savior. COS has parallel runways about 3 miles apart. No problem ! If, upon arrival, there's a monster storm in front of you, just land on the parallel that's in the clear ! I nominate every airport in the good old USA be set up this way, no more ulcers or diversions ! Some airports have all the room ! The next thing we were taxiing to the jet center and finishing the after-clearing checks.

Randy had been psyched for the ride in the Lear. While we were unloading him, he said his dad had owned a Cessna 170 but it sure didn't go like this one. I shot back at him that his dad's plane had about 16,000 less horse power than we had !

His mom and dad greeted us there, thanking us gratefully for the safe delivery of their son. Then we were off to our home base of APA the scenic way ! Air Traffic Control, I think, were breaking in some new controllers who appeared to me to be bungling everything up, making us climb, descend, turn here, and then turn there. Oh well, we all fly because we love it so why not sit back and enjoy what you can't control, right ? In reality we were given these endless vectors for traffic avoidance, and I certainly can't complain about that kind of help from ATC (Air Traffic Control.)

18. CHARLES AND THE BUD MAN

Thursday started with a call from dispatch; we were to relocate 200 miles from our overnight roost at Milwaukee's Mitchell International, across Lake Michigan to Pontiac's Oakland International airport. From there our destination would be south to Titusville, Florida. After getting a weather briefing and filing an instrument flight plan, I preflighted our N102AR, first outside, then completed all of the inside checks, checked ATIS, received my clearance, and then waited for all of the usual medical complications to be sorted out before we could depart.

When the medical arrangements for our future patient were finalized we were given the go-ahead. After a quick 215 mile climb to 23,000 feet and an immediate descent, I was told to descend and maintain 3,000, and to enter a wide left downwind to runway 27 Left and to call when abeam the tower on the south side. It seemed there was other closer-in traffic on the north side using 27 Right, which was a shorter runway for the general aviation guys and gals.

After completing the shut down checks, I set the plane up for the next leg to Titusville, Florida, had her topped off with over three tons of fuel, and called clearance delivery, who replied, "N102 AR is cleared to TIX Space Coast Regional Airport via the Pontiac 8 departure procedure, fly the runway heading, expect radar vectors to CAVVS, direct Waterville, direct Appleton as filed, maintain 3,000 feet, departure is 134.75, squawk 2544.

Our patient, Charles, had been in a very severe car accident up north here in Michigan on the fourth of July and almost died. His wife and three children had flown up commercially from Titusville during his recovery. We were to take them all home today. He had two really smashed legs, a torn liver, and his spleen had been severed. He was in lots of pain. We had a special portable pump that needed to inject exact amounts of morphine into his saline solution during the two-hour flight to Florida.

It was smooth, easy sailing until two hundred miles north of Savannah, where a severe line of thunderstorms had developed and were leaving behind them some much needed rain. Good for them, bad for us. Those big boomers cause havoc to the pilots who need to navigate around them. They're not any fun, to say the least. Actually, it's nerve racking as we pick our way through and around a cluster or line of storms.

Surprisingly, as soon as we crossed into Florida, the storms were no more and our one hundred fifty-mile descent was quite uneventful. Usually the citrus state is full of towering cumulo-nimbus this time of year. But not this time. Cool! Soon we were on the 95 degree humid tarmac of TIX, which is the closest civilian airport to the Kennedy Space Center and Cape Canaveral.

After unloading our patient, his family, and all of our luggage for our overnight stay, I met some of the nicest people in the world. The owners of the fixed base operation (FBO), Tico Aviation, went way out of their way to make our stay more comfortable. They set up the hotel rooms, Fed Ex'd the medical pump back to Pontiac for us, drove us to where ever we wished, and refueled our plane in case we had a trip before they reopened on the following morning. If any of you ever fly into TIX, take my advice and taxi to Tico Aviation !

Guess what happened next ? My room at the Holiday Inn Express was overlooking the Kennedy Shuttle launching facility. Unbelievable ! And if that wasn't exciting enough there was a rocket launch the next morning and the next after that ! Too bad though as I slept completely through the 4 a.m. launch. All of the locals told me the night shuttle launches are an awesome sight. Not only does Titusville light up like it's noontime on a sunny day, but even Orlando which is a good thirty-some miles away.

Old Bud, our taxi cab driver, offered me some fried alligator. At first I was talking my way out of trying it, but decided to be brave and try some. It was great ! Kind of like fried clams, but more tender. I also learned from Bud that the male gator sits on the eggs and young ones, and that alligators rarely attack people; alligators will only attack if they feel threatened. Bud says he swims all the time in the same ponds where the gators live ! He said they hadn't bothered him too much yet, but if an alligator should rise up on all fours and come after you, you know you're in trouble as they can top 35 miles per hour. Then, he says, the only way to survive is to zig-zag as you run for your life as alligators can only run that fast in a straight line. Wow !

Alligators aren't wimps either: An adult male can tip the scales over the 400 pound mark.

Bud also fought in action in both the Viet Nam and Gulf Wars, and maybe that has something to do with alligators not bothering him while he is taking an afternoon swim! Good luck Bud-man !

19. Low Pressure Systems

Hey, I should have written another book in the past week but when I'm so busy flying how can I write ? Here are a few of the week's events that come to mind. The past week was full of 'hard IMC' (instrument meteorological conditions) flying, meaning the low pressure systems caused the clouds to start near the surface with their tops at around 32,000 feet. Add in morning mist and fog, along with heavy rain, and you may see that I earned every cent I was paid this week.

We flew from home base 40 N to Bedford, Massachusetts on Wednesday morning; we flew out of the low pressure disturbance about twenty miles or so before entering the preferred right downwind for runway 29 at the very noise-sensitive city. It was three minutes before 7 a.m.; the tower answered our arrival announcement by saying that if we wanted their services we would have to wait another three minutes as they resume operations every morning precisely at 7 o'clock !

We were VMC (visual meteorological conditions) as I was slowing from 250 to 200 knots on the right downwind for runway 29 when I said to Charlie what in heck is that thing out the front of our windscreen ? Then about one second later it transformed from a mosquito-like looking thing into a Beechcraft Bonanza that was banking hard to his right and I to my right as I think he saw us about the same time as we saw him. A second-and-a-half later he wasn't in front of us any more and the field was ours. We had called at least three times on tower frequency while inbound and had heard nothing but silence in return but still it had been a near miss. I'll bet he landed immediately thereafter to check himself for color-coded underwear !

We departed Bedford at 0800 and flew into terrible conditions landing at New York City's busiest little airport (actually located in New Jersey) called Teterboro (TEB) which is the corporate headquarters' airport for the Big Apple. I remember breaking out into visual conditions at 230 feet above the ground and still could only see the runway lights. The ATIS (automatic terminal information service) was calling visibility at one-half mile at best as we landed there with what I thought to be the cleanest plane in the world considering we had flown through very heavy rain that morning already for almost two full hours ! I had filed Newark as our alternate but to tell the truth I think that had I missed the approach because of weather I would have back-tracked to Windsor Locks, Connecticut; I had already told our two business men passengers prior to leaving Bedford that Windsor Locks would be our landing alternate.

The next issue that comes to mind occurred that same day. The storm system was working towards the northeast all that day and eventually swallowed up the Beantown area too. I flew the ILS 11 to return the guys home to BED, and soon thereafter was informed from dispatch of a major change of plans. Instead of us spending the short enough night as it was there in BED we were to relocate to Philly as my New Orleans trip for the next day had been taken away and replaced with a Philly-to-Lansing, Michigan (LAN) trip that had a show time of 0630 with a wheels-into-the wells time of 0730. Hey, I'm used to changes. No problem. We'll catch the French Corridor on the next pass, right ?

I quickly filed our flight plan to Philly: direct Lucos, Sandy Point, Hampton, Jet 121 Briggs, for the Cedar Lake Seven arrival into PHL. As Charlie Dog attempted to get our clearance five minutes later, we were informed that our destination area was gridlocked due to poor weather and that we could not be released for another 75 minutes. Bummer ! All revved up and no place to go. I took a nap as C. Dog was reading Time magazine. I haven't seen the Dog read anything in eleven months but he was reading tonight.

After an hour passed I refreshed myself with some cold tap water on my face as well as a refreshing brushing of the teeth. I then called and received our clearance and off we blasted. And what a ride we had. The weather was bad, the ride was fair, and the scenery was almost out of this world beautifully breathtaking ! Between Cedar Lake and Dupont on my descent I flew through a mile-long five hundred-foot deep canyon of cloud and soon after that flew through a maybe seventy five-foot diameter blue sky hole in a wall of solid cloud, one of the biggest thrills of the year so far for me.

Soon thereafter I had to fly Philly's ILS to 09 Right to minimums. That was not as bad as the nerves of the controllers on this evening. Air Traffic Control was packing airplanes onto final approach like sardines. Every one was given speeds and altitudes by the minute. "Lear 156 Juliet

Sierra slow from 250 to 190, then descend and maintain four thousand"...as an example and this went on seemingly forever with one request after another. I remember flying in the soup on a right downwind for 09 Right only four miles from the threshold but soon found myself on vectors 28 miles to the southwest as the controller tried to find a break in the arrivals to fit us into ! Finally established on the ILS we soon saw the runway-approach lighting system at about 200 feet; another day of hard concentration was about to end.

The third memory item that pops up in my gray matter happened the following morning on our trip from Philly into Lansing. I remember answering my passengers, as we all boarded the jet, when they asked me if I expected a smooth flight. I shook my head from left to right and said I did not see how it could possibly be a smooth ride as we were flying from one low pressure area into another. The clouds and rain in the bowels of these mammoth systems are one issue but the turbulence aloft for hundreds of miles away is another ! Just as I thought, the ride to Lansing was rougher than a cob, flying outbound from the PHL low, and more of the same flying into the Great Lakes low— sometimes that's just the way things go——but then came our approach.

Cleveland had us descend early into the twenties but then held us there seemingly forever. Finally Lansing Approach told us to intercept the Localizer (the final approach course) for runway 28 and to descend from 10,000 to 3,000 feet, that we were three miles from the final approach fix called Artda and we were cleared for the ILS (Instrument Landing System) to runway 28 Left and to contact the Tower at the marker, good morning.

I turned for the intercept and extended the spoilers as we began almost free falling while slowing from 250 to 200 knots. Very soon we passed the marker, the five-mile final approach fix, while still 3,000 feet too high. I retracted the boards and called flaps 8, then gear down, then flaps 20 and landing checks. Soon we were two miles out and still over 1,000 feet too high when all of a sudden we broke out into visual conditions seeing this beautiful airport with its primary runway directly under us with no chance to land as we were still way too high. Charlie Dog told the tower we needed to execute the missed approach procedure but Tower responded by asking if we could circle to land. I asked Charlie what circling minimums were and he said 1,400 feet. We were in and out of the ragged cloud bases at 1,900 feet so I told him sure, we'd make left traffic for 28 L.

We then descended to 1,400 , circled left and greased the slickest civilian aircraft ever made onto the wet and black Michigan tarmac. I remember the adrenalin rush lasted somewhat longer than the engine whining as we shutdown for the morning.

These are only a few of the many deals that happened this past week. I guess this is why I get such a kick out of this job—there's never a dull moment and every day "is a winding road" full of new adventures and new experiences.

20. Earning our Pay

Everyone and their wife's uncle must have been flying yesterday as I departed 40N for Myrtle Beach.

I was step climbed from 3,000 almost 1,000 feet at a time until finally arriving at 39,000 ! Lots of work. We were cleared originally to Modena, direct Woodstown, Woodstown 198 degree radial to intercept the Salisbury 013 degree radial at Haydo, then direct Salisbury, Jet 209 which is the 211 degree outbound radial from the Salisbury VOR to the Sawed intersection, then direct Norfolk, outbound from there on the 223 degree radial called Jet 121 to Weavr intersection, then direct to the Kinston VOR, and then direct Myrtle Beach—another "simple" clearance—but if you figure in the twenty or so climbs and level-offs associated with those step climbs, plus the bad weather avoidance—you can start to see that sometimes we do earn our pay.

On our way home we had our hands full avoiding all of the cumulus build-ups. The Lear's high weather topping abilities is for naught when Center controllers descend us while we're still so far out—in yesterday's case down into the bowels of some nasty stuff. We were cleared as filed out of Myrtle, direct to the Mulls intersection, then direct to the Tar River VOR, then direct to the Patuxent VOR to then join the Dupont 4 arrival. I started deviating about 100 miles south of Richmond for some storms, which seemed to be popping up right where I needed to go.

After my second deviation Washington told me to let them know when I was ready to copy my new clearance, and from me being used to the great mid-Atlantic airways and from flying a lot in the Northeast, I fired back immediately that I was ready to copy. It turned out I knew everything the controller was going to fire at me before he even spoke ! "November 200 Tango Whiskey is now cleared to the 40 November airport via present position direct to Norfolk, direct Salisbury, Victor 29 Dupont direct, descend now to and maintain flight level 290." I replied back that exact clearance and as we turned to the right for our descent towards Norfolk, I saw another red blob about one hundred miles out on the Radar screen. About eighty miles out I told the next controller that I needed to deviate for some weather eighty miles ahead, and said left 10 degrees would probably keep us closer to staying on course, plus us deviating towards the windward side of the 50 knot winds aloft would give us a better ride too.

"Unable left deviation", the controller shot back to me, and then told me to contact the next sector. Checking in with my usual " Howdy Washington Center, Learjet 200 Tango Whiskey is checking in out of flight level 310 for 290 direct Norfolk; and we need to deviate for weather either way."

"Roger that 200 Tango Whiskey, turn 20 degrees left vectors for the descent, descend and maintain flight level 250."

"Unable 20 left, we have a level 5 storm out there at our 10 o'clock and five zero miles" I fired back. As the minutes pass, you see, the angles and altitudes keep changing what we see, and the weather is changing also.

"Well you cannot deviate right at this point," center told me, and I replied, OK, that will work for us, and I turned a few degrees left and we ended up passing the boomer kind of close.

The ride was a rough one but after we rounded that corner and turned towards Salisbury, I needed three more deviations, all towards the west, before I flew into clearer air. After the third deviation I was cleared direct Terri, Dupont, direct 40 N, but as I was approaching Terri, I was then told to fly direct Modena and plan on holding as there was IFR traffic inbound also to my airport. I and my trusty copilot, Bill Davis, briefed on the holding pattern and soon, about three miles before arriving at Modena I was given a vector to intercept the localizer into Chester County, which voided all other clearances.

By then we were nine miles from the airport and believe me it is quite a chore just keeping track of where you are. Soon I called for flaps 8 degrees and descended to 2,400. For the past thirty minutes, from one hundred miles south of Norfolk, we had been constantly descending and deviating but now as the localizer came alive at six miles out I turned to 293 degrees, called flaps 20 and gear down and landing checks please. Bill did his 'stuff' as we passed Moses the outer marker, glide slope alive, 40 degrees of flap please, as we slid down the air slide until finally breaking out into visual conditions and seeing the runway two miles in front of us, while of course our speed was V Ref (final approach speed based on weight) plus 10 knots with the cross hairs for the ILS nailed perfectly.

I greased the great white Jet onto her home base's tarmac. As I completed the shut down checks I thanked Bill for his usual fine help, and noted also that we had flown a total of only two point three hours but had both indeed earned our daily pay.

21. Hurried Pace

Today's trip to Chicago and back seemed to totally have happened in high gear. Leaving a rainy Chester County and all of its associated turbulence, clouds, and eventually icing above 15,000 feet, we did not enjoy smooth air until crossing the Illinois border. Our ride at FL390 (39,000 feet) was rougher than a cob, and there was no way out of it as it was at all altitudes.

Believe me I heard a lot of whining today. We flew the ILS 04 Right to three miles out when we side stepped and landed on the Left. Our two passengers' stretch-Limo was awaiting as were our fuel truck and the ground power unit. I walked my two passengers through the FBO (fixed base operator's office) to their ride, then checked the weather again back home and was surprised that the ceilings were still above above 2,000 feet.

I hurried the gal in charge of the billing as I wanted to get back home ASAP before our approach would get to minimums or below. "Alright let's see now, $125.00 for a handling fee, $30.00 parking fee, $40.00 GPU fee, and around $1,200.00 for 335 gallons of Jet A." Sign on the dotted line, and run for the door.

"Oh, Captain Van Loan, you must fill out one of these security vouchers—time of arrival, time of departure, how many souls you dropped off, and how many souls are leaving with y'all ?"

I run back for this new post-911 responsibility and after two minutes of almost unreadable hen scratching I'm sprinting towards my great white horse awaiting me, check both fuel caps that they are on correctly, drain the one important belly sump drain, look at all five tires and rims, then look to make sure most parts of each engine appear to be present and normal !

Now, get in, latch the bottom half of the door, then the top half, run the electric motor that engages all twelve of the door locking pins, and then release the hooks when both levers are latched, and call to the other pilot "Two forward" to which he should say "Light's out" if everything is a go as far as the door is concerned. I hop up into the left seat and am briefed as to our initial clearance.

I start the left engine, then the right. The pre-taxi and taxi check lists are completed with military precision as we taxi to 04 Right. Soon we are rocketing towards the distant skyscrapers that fill the wind screen until at 3,000 feet or so we are again in total instrument meteorological conditions.

Soon we are at 41,000 feet and crossing the ground at over 600 miles an hour heading towards Gipper, then Dryer (Cleveland), then direct to Johnstown, Pennsylvania for the Bunts One arrival. A bit over an hour had passed as we flew through heavy rain to the MXE VOR to hold as published, as there was a jet on the ILS ahead of us into 40 N. As we made the first lap in the hold we were cleared for the approach. With our over 20 knot tail wind, circling to land on the opposite runway was a must, and at 700 feet above the ground we broke out to a maybe two mile visibility as I turned right and made left traffic for 11.

With all of that turbulence and rain, believe me when I tell you I had a handful of airplane and I remember telling Charlie just that, to which he yelled "I'll bet you do," showing his usual huge grin ! I had gone to full flaps on the ILS but as I broke off that approach to circle I called for flaps 20 for the circle and configured her back to 40 degrees of landing flaps while on my base-to-final turn. The wind shear was all of 20 knots on final and as I cleared the runway I noticed a bit of shaking going on—from inside of me !

We shut everything down and went inside to finish all of the paperwork. I was then informed that I have a ten-day gig and it's mostly out west. Great, but I am somewhat bummed out over losing my Yellowstone vacation. Oh well, I'll be in Aspen at least twice next week and that will be nice if the weather cooperates. Also on the agenda are cities such as Baltimore, Boston, Cleveland, Denver, Houston, Denver again, Aspen, Denver again, Indianapolis, Denver again, Aspen again, on up to Green Bay, then home.

By then I'll be pushing for some days off so I can get to my Upstate N.Y. home and return to being a farmer for a few days.

22. Never Ending Adventures

I remember last night as I rotated 157 Juliet Sierra my eyes immediately lowered and focused to the inside of the cockpit and the glass instruments that would guide me solely for the next 12 minutes. We had just departed Detroit City Airport's runway 15 and it was raining hard. The radar would not paint on the ground, but as soon as the wheels were up she painted nicely—if you can call flying into such conditions nice. We had spent the last ten hours in Detroit and Charlie and I wanted to get home for sure, the sooner the better.

OK, runway heading to 3,000 feet; at 1,000 feet we had all the after take-off checks done and I had already accelerated to 250 knots as the digital instantaneous vertical speed indicator approached 7,000 feet per minute climb rate, and as I saw 2,000 feet slip by on the right side digital altitude tape I pulled the power back somewhat to around

700 degrees Centigrade per side until a second later and within 700 feet of target altitude I started pushing the yoke forward and trimming the pitch trim button forward so as to magically stop our ascent at the designated 3,000 feet.

As all this was happening ATC said to turn left 20 degrees for vectors for the climb and to climb to and maintain one zero thousand (ten thousand). As I was hearing this I smoothly pulled back on the yoke while my left thumb was now pulling the pitch trim button rearward and my right hand was adding power while my eyes scanned quickly and efficiently from one task at hand to another: Left wing down 20 degrees; pitch to 15 degrees; nose up; power up to 795 degrees; stop the bank now at 20 degrees; here comes that new heading; vertical speed rising to 8,000 feet per minute which is OK but what's the airspeed now doing? It's decreasing slightly so—pitch trim and push ahead slightly; OK everything is now in perfect sync—but here comes 10,000 so we need to level off; but now ATC says after passing 10,000 we could proceed right direct to the Wings intersection and to continue the climb to Flight level 230. OK, leave the power alone, right turn 40 degrees to Wings, re-tilt the radar as we climb: "Charlie how does the picture of this weather look to you?" The turbulence is quite nasty but the painted sweeps looks like it's only rain with no convective activity.

So we continue this climb and I turn on the nacelle heats as the outside air temps approach freezing. But wait, 157JS has a total air temperature (TAT) digital indicator and I'm used to the ram air temperature (RAT) indicator so I press the selector's indicator button and see the Static Air Temperature which says plus 3 degrees; so right way I turn on the Wing and Stabilizer Anti-ice switch and our ears quickly tell us it is working correctly as the cabin pressure 'bumps' less momentarily. It's funny how you can get used to certain gauges and all of a sudden you realize that the indicator you're now looking at is trying to tell you something that you are not processing correctly. In this case I should have had all of the anti-ice 'on' as we approached 10 degrees of 0 degrees Centigrade, but the darned gauge defaults to Total Outside Air Temp instead of Static or Ram Air Temp, if you will, so I always need to know in one way, shape or form if the temperature on my flying surfaces is conductive to building ice or not, period. Of course we only use this bleed air to heat the surfaces when we need to as the engine temps will rise, and thrust out of the tail cone decreases while using anti-ice.

We were still climbing through visible moisture until finally at 32,000 feet we broke out into a clear star-filled sky. There was no moisture at this altitude, so the anti-ice switches were all turned off and we climbed on up leveling at FL390. I left the thrust as it was set for the climb and accelerated to Mach 0.80 which gave us just 700 mph across the ground. After this I adjusted the thrust back some to 550 pounds of fuel flow per side per hour and enjoyed the next thirty minutes we had until landing back at Northeast Philly. I shut down the left engine and Charlie walked two passengers into the terminal as I received our next clearance to 40N.

Back in the plane and securing the entrance door once again, Charlie and I had some more work before we were done for the evening. After blasting off from PNE's runway 6, I flew a climbing left 180 up to 3,000 feet for vectors to the ILS 29 back into Chester County. The ASOS (automatic surface observation system) was calling winds from the east at 11 knots, gusting to 20 knots, so as I approached a three-mile final for 29 and at 2,200 feet, I broke the approach off to the right and entered a left downwind for 11.

Soon thereafter Charlie Dog and I, along with our last passenger, were deplaning once again. And today starts a week's worth of never ending adventures on the road.

23. Instrument Flight Rules Departure

My day today started badly right from the beginning. I arrived at the office and checked the weather at Wilmington, Delaware where I was to pick up my passengers. To my surprise Wilmington's best runway was closed for construction, and their ILS to runway 1 was also out of service. I checked out their other instrument approaches and figured maybe I could 'get in' alright on their VOR approach to runway 9, but soon thereafter I saw another notice that limited airplanes from landing on that runway to less than 12,500 pounds which meant we were not allowed to land on it. The weather was also lower than the lowest altitude allowed on this approach, so we called the passengers and told them we couldn't pick them up there.

After a few more phone calls they decided to drive to Chester County where we were and that we'd depart out of home base. By the time they arrived the weather home had worsened with a cloud height of about 30 feet and a visibility of around 800 feet. We loaded everyone onboard and I got to work up in my office as usual. As my new copilot Brian closed the hatch, he asked me if I had seen the take-off of the airplane in front of us. I said no and asked why. He said the pilot had pitched his nose attitude really high and as he got up maybe 30 feet in the air he nosed over to a level attitude and disappeared into the soup. I said, "I wonder why anyone would fly like that in such weather?"

Brian then briefed our passengers and hopped up into the cockpit next to me. With the engines now running I turned on our avionics master switch to discover my primary EADI would not come online. We proceeded to trouble-shoot but could not get the radio to perform properly, so I shut everything down and told the passengers we needed to switch planes as this one was not airworthy but that we could probably be departing in thirty minutes or so in our sister ship. They agreed to this plan and back we went into the terminal building. That's when the phone call came.

Philly approach called us and asked if the plane that had departed in front of us had made an emergency landing back at our field. Heck no, we all said, there was no way anyone could land here as the weather was extremely low. The next call came a few minutes later. The plane that had departed in front of us had crashed a few miles from the end of the runway and everyone onboard was killed. Also it had crashed into a house or some houses in a nearby development.

The next thing, my lead passenger came up to me and said that they didn't feel like flying today and they were canceling the trip, and all three of them walked out the door. I cancelled my fuel order for my second plane, finished my paperwork and headed for home. The day had been one big headache for me thus far but was still so much better than the day was for the people and the plane that departed in front of us.

24. TWENTY FIVE HOUR WEEK

So much to tell and no time for telling. That's the way this past how many days has been. What day is it anyway? I just glanced at the last two pages in my ninth logbook and I see I've flown 25 hours in this past week. I know, all of you worked over 40 hours last week so y'all don't want to hear how hard we Captains have it, right ? And come on, a 25-hour work week is something all Americans dream about having, right ? And besides, for so few working hours per week our kind are just traveling around this great country visiting really cool places, as if we're on some perpetual vacation of our own, right ? Well, yeah, it is sort of—kind of—like that. Some of the time anyway.

Wednesday I flew to South Bend from home and then on out to Jackson Hole. Getting there nonstop from SBN was a big concern and also was the weather we would encounter there upon arriving. I climbed to 45,000 feet initially and soon requested the block altitude flight level 450 to flight level 470. As I burned fuel I climbed so as to conserve fuel. I tried to keep our true airspeed around 420 knots, though sometimes you can get so involved in conserving your fuel burn that you end up not flying as fast as a Learjet should fly. So many variables in this business !

Upon reaching 47,000 feet and while enjoying the new-to-me views from this lofty perch while cruising over Pierre and then Rapid City, South Dakota, I saw my fuel burns settle on 414 pounds per engine per hour. My true airspeed was still 420 knots and the curvature of the earth in front of me was absolutely astounding. What a difference from my usual 41,000 to 43,000 foot cruise picture was this 47,000 footer ! The problem of climbing higher at this time was the outside air temperature. I saw we were standard temperature plus three degrees, which makes climbing difficult. Colder is better, and three degrees makes all of the difference in the world. Forty seven thousand five hundred feet was all I would get today. But soon, when everything cooperates, I will be cruising at fifty one thousand feet for my first time, calculating economy at that height. I've read that a Lear 31 is cheaper to travel in at 51,000 feet than a Ford Explorer is (or is it Exploder as Drew used to call them?) We'll see.

Two hundred miles out from JAC I called flight service and learned of our arrival weather. Thunderstorms and snow showers were all around my destination. I learned also that the winds were from the south favoring their ILS to runway 18. I studied the instrument approach plate well with Pete. Fuel at arrival time would be 1,500 pounds instead of 1,000 pounds because of my lofty fuel-saving cruise profile. We descended through some very nasty cumulo-nimbus and also through moderate icing conditions.

Weather is always worse in the mountains and believe me the Tetons make some of the worst flying conditions imaginable. At around 14,000 feet I saw a big hole off our right side so we cancelled IFR, hit the spoilers and descended into visual conditions; then with power at flight idle and spoilers extended, still flew southbound through one of the most beautiful valleys in this world leading from Yellowstone Lake to the runway. Cool. Breathtaking. Majestic. Awesome.

Our passengers arrived as the fuel truck was driving away from us and in 30 minutes we were climbing back up into the icy overcast. We landed back at Sioux Falls for some leg stretching and fuel and at 1900 hours landed at 40 N. Trip totals were eight air hours even. Work day was fourteen hours. I then finished paperwork and headed home for bed.

Thursday morning came all too quickly and soon Pete and I were headed to Naples, Florida for the second time in four days. Thunderstorms were thicker than fleas on a hound dog in Tennessee in August from southern Georgia to central Florida. This was the first big day for me in thunderstorm avoidance since the end of November of last year. We picked our way through the 200 mile mess and things went pretty well. The jet stream across central Florida was 157 knots in strength flowing across the Gulf and blew a lot of the turbulence from these 45,000 foot monsters in our path as we flew by some storms on their leeward side. In spite of those bumps things went well and we landed at APF safe and sound.

Again, ten minutes after landing my passengers arrived early and in thirty minutes we were climbing northward over Orlando and back into the thick lines of storms. Nothing like going through a bad thing twice in two hours ! I kept the seatbelt sign on until we were north of Brunswick, Georgia when we flew into the clear.

I had climbed to 43,000 and was given a block to 45,000. I settled in nicely at 44,500 and began collecting data. I then descended to 43,500 and collected more data. On this day in these conditions 44,500 was the choice altitude for economy. I was getting 0.440 air nautical miles per pound of fuel. At 43,000 I was getting 0.423 air nautical miles per pound of fuel. This difference here was 17/1000th of an air nautical mile per pound of fuel which is about 102 feet of distance more per air nautical mile per pound of fuel. While over North Carolina with 400 nautical miles to go, this means I could 'save' 40,800 feet if I flew at 44,500 instead of at 43,000 feet which converts to 6.8 miles saved which converts to about a one minute savings in time which converts also to about thirty bucks saved.

Time is money in this world so here I am trying my best to save my customers time and money. What I also figured was since my true air speed stayed at 450 knots while collecting this data that this minute saved was also that famous penny earned.

So be it. I am always trying to save. But no two flights are alike because of temperature, weight, pressure, jet streams, thunderstorms, phases of the moon and a million other factors. So every day is a winding road full of new adventures ! So I ask you all again, who could possibly work more than 25 hours a week with all of this excitement going on ?

25. COORDINATION FROM ALL

I had repositioned from Coatesville to New Haven, Connecticut, awaiting our young passenger who had hired us to whisk him to Freeport, Bahamas. At 4 p.m. dispatch called and told me the passenger called them and said he was running a little late. At 5 p.m. they called again and said it looked like he would be there no later than 6:30 p.m. This was fine with me but probably wouldn't be so fine with the Customs and Immigrations Officials on the Island. I then took care of updating the US Customs outbound officials; they'd have no problems with this flight running late, unlike the Bahamas inbound people.

Around 7 p.m. we loaded Steve and his bags while clearance delivery cleared us to Mike Yankee Golf Fox (MYGF) airport via the Bridgehaven Five departure procedure, radar vectors Beads, direct Emjay, Jet 174 Dixon, Atlantic Route 7 Adoor, direct. Climb to 2,000. Expect

45,000 in 10 minutes, departure this evening is 126.95, and squawk 6613.

As I scrambled to enter all of the routing into 156JS's Universal Navigation Systems computer, I couldn't help but smile with appreciation of the fact that with each and every fix that is entered one can simply press— say, for instance, the airways 'line select' button, and every airway that is associated with that last fix selection will be listed, so that all I have to do is push the correct button and the complete airway will be selected into the navigation computer as far as I want to go on that particular airway. There, with one button I saved maybe five minutes of scrambling through a map and another five minutes of trying to find, spell and enter all of the many intersections that are present.

Not only will this box navigate, but it displays my entire flight course on an 8-inch TV screen in the center of the cockpit for both pilots to view with their heads up instead of looking down at a map; that is a huge additional safety feature. This course is displayed in various mileage ranges from a few to 600 miles, if you wish to see that far ahead. I usually keep the range at 150 miles. However, if we are using the weather radar also, range is limited to 300 miles, with 150 the maximum distance to really see what is going on ahead as far as radar returns.

While flying using the radio detection and ranging device (radar) I usually scan ahead using the 50 to 100 mile ranges. Also, at the touch of a button, one can add to the display VORs, NDBs and airports; and if you touch the appropriate button a second time you'll get more of them; touch it a third time and they disappear. It's like seeing anything in front of you including, of course, 45 degrees either side of center that you may wish to look at. These features are extremely helpful, to say the least.

Soon after departing HVN we were radar identified and cut corners quickly to Emjay, and soon after with Washington Center we were direct Dixon NDB which sits next to Wilmington, North Carolina and has been in use for a long time guiding airplanes, and probably sailors also, from there to and through the Islands. I remember being 200 miles north of ILM when we were cleared direct to Adoor, and that put us out into the Atlantic quite far, too far for gliding to land if both engines quit, especially against our 160 knot crosswind from the west. I had told Charlie that I was concerned about a frontal system that had played havoc in Florida earlier this day. As we passed abeam Cape Fear, I called Washington Flight Watch on the appropriate frequency for a weather update. After explaining to the weather specialist exactly where I was and where I was going, he advised me of the now two clusters of thunderstorms, the first east of the Ormond Beach area and the second east of West Palm Beach. After much discussion, I decided if I needed to deviate for the storms I would deviate left for the first batch and maybe also eastward for the second cluster of storms.

As our radar was within 150 or so miles, I could see that my planning was correct. I told Air Traffic Control I needed 15 degrees left for the next 100 miles which we did. Then the picture began to get interesting. After this 100 mile diversion, my direct to destination line looked best at first if I also deviated east from the approaching secondary storm system, but then I saw I would be downwind from several 43,000 foot high thunderstorms with the same 100-plus-knot crosswind pushing all that nasty stuff right towards me, and guess what? Turbulence as well as everything else flows down hill or down wind, so I cut a course 20 degrees to the right or to the west of Freeport which was now only 200 miles away, in order to stay upwind of that problem and we passed this cluster by a good fifteen miles or so to the west.

OK, now that I had the storm problems at bay, I redirected my steed to my destination. I had made a deal with Miami Center that if they let me stay at altitude until I had finished deviating, I would give them a good descent rate when I was ready. Dealing, you see, is a huge part of flying the system as well as being a big part in our every day lives. If you let me do this, then I'll give you that kind of thing. ATC professionals deal constantly. They have their guidelines and protection bubbles around each and every Instrument Flight Rules airplane that cannot be penetrated with any other traffic. However, lots of times one plane can climb some, and another can descend some, and everyone will be happy. This also goes for speeding up or slowing down to help others. Of course I will always offer to step it up a notch or two but sometimes I am asked to slow down which always makes my upper lip start to curl.

Anyways, I needed better than 3,000 feet per minute and Miami turned us over to what they phrased as Grand Bahamas Approach Control who immediately cleared us from present position direct to RAPPS, then direct to the VOR, and plan to cross Rapps at 7,000 feet and the VOR at 1,500 feet. Up came the spoilers and down we floated through 10,000 feet where I needed to slow from 325 knots of indicated airspeed to the mandatory 250 knots below 10,000 feet, pretty much a universal speed restriction. We hit Rapps at exactly 7,000 and called it for a position report as their approach control is armed with only a radio and binoculars !

The next thing I remember was her (Approach Control) asking us if we had the Plates for the ILS to runway 6, and as we replied yes, she cleared us directly to the outer marker compass locater, to 1,500 feet, and also cleared us for the approach. Things were happening more quickly than usual, partly due to our need for the weather topping which delayed our descent. Believe me, anytime it takes more than a 3,000 foot per minute descent while navigating for an arrival and subsequent approach, we two pilots in the front are very busy campers indeed. I saw ten miles from the airport and then two miles as I tracked to the LOM (locater outer marker of the instrument landing system which is usually about 5 miles out from the landing threshold on the extended runway centerline) which was super imposed on my EHSI (electronic horizontal situation indicator) and as we broke out of the soup I said to Charlie Dog to look at all those lights over on my side.

It was a long row of white lights that looked kind of like maybe a runway. Just as I said this the Lady Controller asked us if we had the field in sight yet. I guess she saw us with her binoculars at about the same time we saw her airport. As I reconfirmed bearing and distance I said yes, the airport was indeed in sight. She must have been working approach, tower and ground too as she cleared us for landing at that moment. I remember looking up and seeing 258 knots on my airspeed and I was abeam the landing threshhold on a one-mile real tight left downwind.

Charlie became extremely busy completing the approach and before-landing checks, as this was the first moment in the past 100 nautical miles that I had stopped my 3,000 FPM descent rate and was leveling at 1,500 feet. I then threw the spoilers to the air once again as I trimmed nose-up attitude and pulled the control column aft; as I saw 258 knots dwindle to 180, I stowed the boards and put out flaps 8 and gear down as I turned left base. Charlie was nearing completion of his vocally aloud checks as I added flaps 20 and kept her turning as we rolled out on a 1.5 mile final at 140 knots of speed. Charlie was caught up with me and I with him as I asked for landing flaps and fence checks, please, and the next five seconds were spent calling airspeed and rechecking the checks until once again, we chirp, chirp and chirped onto the 87-degree Bahamian tarmac, ending yet another spectacular flying evening filled with the kinds of adventures and challenges and excitement that seem to keep inviting me back for more, day after day.

Not only is the flying part the greatest part of each day, but also the coordination involved for each flight is simply amazing. Coordination between crew and machine. Coordination between controllers and crew. Coordination between airplanes sharing the heavens. And let us not forget the one most important of all—the cockpit crew coordination which usually performs as marvelously as the Learjet itself.

26. Grumbling Old Dogs

Sunday was another spectacular, sunny, 85 ish degree early March kind of day in the Bahamas. Charlie Dog and I spent the morning in the shade of trees and umbrellas on the southern coastline of Freeport's Westin Resort area, reminiscing of days of old as well as planning for the future. We both came to the conclusion that we wouldn't change too much of the past even if we could do so, but it sure would have been nice had we some of the brains back when we started as what we had by now. It seems that while we relaxed and reminisced we both agreed that we had lolly gagged along the winding path of life that led us to this shady spot where we now sat. Charlie and I are best of friends and we fly together often.

I had gone to Cornell University on a special one year Ag program after graduating from high school with a regents diploma, and then came back to the only life I had ever known and started my working career in 1973 with a wife, son, and parents on a large dairy farm.

Charlie had his high school diploma in his hand as he jumped into that new Cherokee 150 and soon held private, instrument, commercial and flight instructor ratings. He was immediately hired for pay to instruct and soon he had built enough hours to actually fly some part 135 single engine gigs with paying customers. Soon thereafter he was hired by the Commuters and has spent the last 27 years flying people around in Turbo props and Hawker Jets. I had farmed until 1993 when we sold the cows, machinery and half the land; then I began flight training in hopes of some day being privileged enough to fly people around and to even be paid for such. This was only a dream in 1995. By 1997 I had earned a flight instructor certificate and had built some 2,200 hours; then I was given the opportunity to fly Learjets for a living in the spring of 1999. Here I sat in the shade and listened to Charlie as he spoke of my flying abilities. He told me that he has flown every kind of little airplane ever built as well as Airbuses and Boeing 727s, 737s, 757s and even 747s with many of the best pilots around, and that I and my friend Ken were the two best pilots he had ever flown with, bar none.

I said, oh come on now, stop the BS, but he said it wasn't bull at all, that I was a real pilot flying the hardest airplane to fly he had ever seen. He also said the reason I am as good as I am is because not only do I want to be that good but because I started my Jet career in the Learjet which is as difficult to fly as they get.

Charlie then told how lately he has had the chance to type in the 747 and 757 but that he doesn't want to be away from home from his seven-year-old daughter, wife and parents with that kind of an 'on the road so much' job. Charlie always says bigger airplanes mean bigger suitcases !

So he is flying with me and wants to get typed in the Lear jet.

I laugh when he talks about my abilities as I have never flown any other type of jet. But he insists I know how to really fly and any other career move into any other type of jet would be an easy one. He also tells me daily that the Lear is a slippery, unforgiving airplane that can and will bite to kill if you let her, and again I just grin at him as I know of no other way.

Soon local time was nearing 15:00 and we had an 18:00 departure time for a 21:00 hour local arrival time in New Haven with a clearing customs stop in Wilmington, N.C. at 19:30. We checked out of the Westin, and Godfrey the cab driver was right on time for our ten-minute ride to the airport. I had completed all of my Customs, Immigrations and APIS (advanced passenger information service) paperwork two days prior and this should prove to be an enjoyable and uneventful evening flight home, or so I thought.

Five minutes after getting into my preflight, Charlie came out to the plane and said the client called and wanted to leave at 5 instead of 6 o clock and that he wished to bring three unexpected (to us) friends along also for the ride back home. I called dispatch and said it would be OK but that they needed to rearrange customs and APIS for me and to fax all paperwork back to me as I, as Captain and Pilot-in-Command, am ultimately responsible for everything.

With finally the preflight done as well as the fueling, I filed the international flight plan and the next two domestic legs after ILM. The briefer told me of some very nasty weather along my route to ILM just as it had been two days prior when I had flown into here. The plan this time seemed an easterly diversion would be appropriate as the line of storms trailed from Adoor all the way back to Florida's west coast. The other issue was I could not top the weather as I'd be on my climb as I entered it. So far, so good. Complex flights must be taken with small steps, one step at a time. You shouldn't worry about things down the pike until you get to them. With the passengers all aboard and the last two faxes in hand, Charlie and I started turning lots of money into noise, and ten minutes after gear-up we were climbing through some very rough weather and deviating to the east as planned.

The turbulence was not nice, it never is, and finally after a rough ride from 15,000 feet it began to smooth out at 35,000 as we finished climbing through the clear nighttime heavens up to our filed flight level of 43,000 feet. Once level and stable, I was surprised to see a head wind component of 50 knots, as we had had the same two days prior on the leg to Freeport. Some days you just can't seem to win. But Wilmington's weather was better than 5,000 and 5 (no clouds below 5,000 feet and better than 5 miles visibility) as we landed straight in on runway 35, clearing the far end for customs.

I had called the Aeronautics Fixed Base Operator (the guy who sells fuel, catering, hangar space, etc.) on the radio from twenty minutes out and had asked him to advise customs of our arrival time and also that once clearing was complete, I would like a ground power unit (GPU) hooked to my plane as well as 400 gallons of go juice .

Customs was very thorough, and twenty minutes later we had been cleared back into the USA. Fueling was in progress, as well as catering gathered and clearance received to New Haven: direct to Norfolk, direct Sea Isle Jet 121 Hampton, direct, maintain ten thousand, expect flight level 330 in ten minutes, departure on 25 and a quarter, squawk 4478.

Off we blasted into the clear star-filled nighttime sky and once on course, we flew for the next hour marveling at the East Coast sights. We could see almost 200 miles in any direction. As we passed every city and the lights, Charlie and I took turns orienting each other as to what this was down here and what that was over there as well as those bridges over yonder. I said to Charlie Dog that I would have done much better in geography had they taught me from such a classroom as this one we were enjoying so much up here at this time.

I was surprised at how many boats and ships were offshore over 50 miles. I believe some of the clusters were commercial or sport fishing boats as one such congregation had 23 ships. I wondered if any of them were looking up at our lights too as we sped northward at over 700 miles an hour across the grounds and waters. Charles W. thought the 23 boat flotilla was located where the ocean floor dropped off sharply, and some sort of fish must have been running there tonight. He has owned many boats through the years and kept some of them on the ocean near where the Delaware Bay meets the Atlantic Ocean near Sea Isle. He said the big boys fish way out there where the floor drops off sharply.

Washington, Baltimore, Philly, Atlantic City were slipping by as the Big Lights were filling the windscreen. We saw several 747s nearby as we descended to the east of Islip, Farmingdale and Kennedy onto the Localizer of New Haven's runway 02 for a landing there at 21:00 hours local. We were right on time to the minute.

I walked the passengers through the gate and to their car as everything was closed up already on this Sunday night, while Charlie got our clearance from New Haven Ground Control. I had tanked enough fuel at ILM for this last leg also, and it's a good thing as no one was here to buy fuel from had we needed any. Clearance was again to 2,000 feet via the Bridge Haven 5 departure procedure, radar vectors to Beads, V 139 to Brigs for the Cedar Lake 7 arrival back home. Again we back-tracked out over the water as that is the way ATC (air traffic control) likes to route the jets.

The southern part of Victor 139 starts at the Hamptons and goes more less to Sea Isle, New Jersey in a semi-straight line and you actually are maybe forty miles offshore abeam New York harbor until you hit Brigs just north of ACY and turn inland there eventually past Philly and on towards our own Chester County Airport.

Atlantic City was absolutely breath-taking to see on this crystal clear night from our only 16,000 foot high ATC limited cruising altitude. It truly is the city of bright lights and glamour of the East—just as Las Vegas is of the West.

Our descent was initiated as I tried to get some night time pictures of the toy sized cities below. Philly was still bustling with arrivals and departures as we were threaded through the busy Class B airspace and onto our own Localizer to runway 29.

Chirp, chirp and chirp was heard once again. Three minutes later the only sounds that could be heard on our home base ramp on this frigid Coatesville night were unwinding gyros, the loud ticking sounds of cooling engine burner cans and the grumbling from two older pilots that were once again safely home but shivering and complaining that winter was still here in the Northeast.

27. Many Variables

Yesterdays flight from Coatesville (40N) to Jackson Hole (JAC) and back to 40N presented many challenges, the first question being can we make it out there non-stop. All of my flight planning figures said we could not make it there and still land with IFR reserves—the 1,200 pounds of fuel that eliminates the notorious pucker factor for us pilots. My estimates all said we would land with only 600 pounds which is of course unacceptable.

As funny as this may sound, I sometimes feel as though I'm an explorer, a test pilot, an adventurer, especially on these kinds of days because no one had ever flown this trip before on this day and under these exact conditions. Just as there are no two alike snowflakes there are no two alike days for two exact trips from our east coast to Jackson Hole. There are many variables on each trip such as taxiing times, holding for release times, vectoring us all over the place times, times being held down 'low' in the teens, times associated from take-off to leveling off at 41,000 feet, as well as the winds and temperatures aloft. These many variables make a non-stop flight either a possibility or a 'could have been' or a 'should have been' or—a has been !

Since we left at 6 a.m. our ground time was minimal and our flight times to Modena, Pottstown, Suzie, Ravine and Badger were also minimal. However, since we entered the 'soup' at 100 feet requiring full anti-ice, this situation probably negated any short cuts that Air Traffic Control had offered us, as a jet uses some of its energy supplying hot bleed air to the leading edges of her wings and tail as well as to the engine front nacelle frames. Our climb seemed to take forever as with full fuel and full anti-ice on we probably averaged only 3,000 feet per minute climb rate to 34,000 feet where we finally broke out of the soup, put on our sun glasses and turned off our anti-ice. There was also a temperature inversion where I noticed the temps never changed from the minus 2 at lift-off till we were well up into the 20's ! I remember tapping my indicated ram air temperature gauge as I thought it had stuck there at minus two degrees.

Leveling off at 410 and finally talking to Cleveland Center, we were bucking an 80-knot head wind until around Dryer (Cleveland) where our ground speed improved somewhat. I told Charlie Dog that I was going to teach him all about long range cruise in Learjets today.

Out came the Pilot Operating Handbook (POH) and as soon as the outside air temperatures and our weight coincided with the charts, I would adjust my thrust settings and altitudes as needed to achieve optimal long-range cruise performance. Our charts are organized to supply to us new figures with each 500 pound weight decrease (due to burning fuel) and also with new power settings for each set of tables. Finally around Green Bay I was level at 43,000 feet and the rest of this 'experimental' trip would be flown at this altitude but with various power settings as we burned fuel and became lighter.

Charlie checked the weather at five airports ahead of us, from Green Bay westward in case we needed to refuel. Things were looking good over northern Iowa and on into South Dakota. By Sioux Falls, I had the Dog tell ATC (air traffic control) that we were changing our destination to Jackson Hole, because I had originally filed to Rapid City for our fuel stop.

"Roger that, November 200 Tango Whiskey. You are now cleared present position direct Jackson Hole, maintain flight level 430," was the reply.

As we flew along the weather improved from a solid undercast, giving way to clear skies. I took three pictures of Mount Rushmore as we flew almost directly overhead. I had to really bank the plane to even see the patriotic granite but the pictures did not really come out that great from so high up. I left 430 at exactly 100 miles out and landed on runway 18 twelve minutes later.

After I cleared the runway and shut down on the ramp I saw the flight's totals. The time was 4 hours and 12 minutes. Fuel burn was 4,600 pounds and my fuel onboard was 1,600 pounds. I had bettered my estimated flight time by 12 seconds but more amazingly I had bettered my estimated fuel burns by a whopping 1,000 pounds by strictly adhering to my long-range cruise tables.

Of course in reality I know it was not just me that had beaten anything on this particular morning's flight, it was me sorting through these everyday variables with much guidance from our Almighty above.

28.   MARSHY ARRIVAL

The problems were mounting rather quickly. We departed Wilmington, North Carolina on a heading of 170 degrees to track to Panal, then Nucar, then direct to Marsh Harbor in the Abacos, the most northerly group of islands in the Bahamas chain. Marsh Harbor lay 450 miles across the water as we dodged thunderstorms enroute. Ken was busy for that hour trying to collect weather information for our destination and for alternates of Vero Beach and Freeport, Bahamas. Nassau would also work in a pinch. As I started my 120 mile descent leaving Flight Level 430 while sipping oxygen, the radar screen was warning me of unpleasant arrival conditions.

The islands were still 120 miles out while we had weather starting around 60 miles and continuing as we painted lots of yellows and reds. As we descended through 25,000 feet the turbulence and icing became moderate to severe in heavy precipitation. Full anti-ice was working overtime as I tried to steady my steed with sweaty hands, keeping enough power to keep my life-supporting bleed air flowing into my cabin, windscreen, wings, tail and engine nacelles, yet reducing power enough trying to descend at least 3,500 feet per minute so as to get to a more user-friendly altitude.

Usually in storms you don't want to be between 20 and 25 thousand feet as that's where the might of the beast is often found. I remember finally throwing up the spoilers and adding power for more bleed air until we found ourselves around 6,000 feet with a glimpse here and there of ground contact. There were heavy rain showers all around and a 1,000 foot above-the-sea broken layer of cloud. I told Ken to cancel IFR and we'd try to get in. You have to cancel before leaving between 5 and 7 thousand feet or air traffic control can't hear you out near the islands. Sometimes there may be another aircraft above somewhere so that he may relay the cancellation, as well as helping us to receive our clearance when we want to leave, but you never know who, if anyone, will be above you for such a relay. All of the Air Traffic Control facilities are based in Florida and their radar and radios only work down to around 5,000 to 7,000 feet from that far away, you see.

Things, at first, while descending out of 5,000 feet looked alright but that low layer of scud was looking thicker and at 10 miles out from the harbor I could see nothing but darkening conditions over that way. We figured we needed to descend to 800 feet to get below the layer which we did. I had slowed to 180 knots and had Ken give me 8 degrees of flaps. I planned on landing towards the east on runway 9, so I started flying a bit towards the west from my southerly flight path so I would have some room to turn 90 degrees left upon seeing our runway that lays in the midst of a piney woods. As Ken called three miles out from our destination I called for 20 degrees of flaps, gear down and landing checks as I flew the jet more and more to the right of course so as to have enough room to turn 90 degrees to the left for our final approach. We were flying by now in extremely heavy rain and at 400 feet above the water.   Ken kept calling degrees from us and distances to our airport. At around one mile I began seeing the cut in the woods and was surprised at how close I was to the end of the runway from which I still had to turn about 90 degrees to the left in order to land.

I called for full flaps and Fence Checks as all of my knowledge and experiences from the past twelve years were riding on the next ten seconds of maneuvering. At times like these I'm running on auto and by feel as there's no time for thinking aloud and analyzing the situation. I remember seeing my V-ref speed plus 20 knots as I banked her quite sharply left to line up with 09 as I descended the last 300 feet. Two seconds later I remember hearing Ken say that we had it made.

The wheels greased onto the flooded hot tarmac as I threw the spoilers up and stood on the brakes. I reached up and also turned on full windshield heat as I could hardly see through the heavy rain. It wasn't over yet and I knew this—with this much rain we could have problems stopping in our usual distance. My anti-skid worked properly as I could feel it brake, release, brake, release, brake, release until I was finally exiting the strip with rubber legs working my rudder pedals .

It must have been a good ten minutes before Ken or I could relax and even talk about the arrival. Then he commented that we had done everything right and it was "The Perfect Approach!" However it did take several more moments for the shaking to turn into smiling for both of us !

29.   Paradise and Hell

I'm not quite awake yet but here it goes. Incredible.
Tropical. Expensive. These are the first three words
that come to mind when I think of my Cayman Island
excursion. Oh, I also think of Cuba and SAMS, but
that's my pilot's brain talking to me. Grand Cayman is the
most populated of the three Cay Islands, but if you have a
small charter airplane or a boat you could visit the other
two very under-developed and primitive islands. It is truly
a tropical paradise and just like Gilligans Island, including
lots of Gingers, Mary Janes, and who were the rich folks ? I
guess I would be the Skipper although I probably act more
like Gilligan (only kidding).

I walked the famous Seven Mile Beach from south to
north but never entered Hell. Seven Mile Beach is on the
western side of Grand Cayman, and the town of Hell is to
the north of the beach on the island's tip. The temps were a

trifle warm for this old country farm boy; I should rephrase that—the humidity was a trifle high for this old country farm boy, and temps varied everyday from nightly lows of 78 to daily highs of 85, except for when I approached the gates of Hell it became way too hot and I had to turn back. I'll be picking out these white grains of paradise for a week from my toes and...? Highlights for me were the Blow Holes. On the eastern side of this British West Indies Isle, the coral reefs protect the island's edges, and in a few places the waves slam onto the high rising coral and where there is an escape channel facing upwards, the force of the seas is redirected vertically and upwards—on the two days I was there maybe to a height of 25 feet ! The loud noise of each geyser made us two old farmers—Charlie and I—goofy acting; we'd laugh and giggled like Mom's cat after a catnip binge ! And yes the Nikon was very busy shuttering, I'll bet 400 times in 3 days ! The food was great and the local Chefs are the best especially when it comes to the jerked or blackened Mahi-Mahi catch of the day. The Island is home to thousands of mixed-breed chickens that I'll bet control the bug problems and keep the 30,000 occupants well fed on the 7-by-20-mile chunk of real estate. Come to think of it I never saw one bug at all !

I rented a small—as in very small—car and we toured the island twice. Of course we snorkeled twice to see the amazing numbers of tropical fish, and the coral which is the reason most people come here as it is rated "number 2" in the world for best places for diving, only second to Australia's famed Great Barrier Reef. The coral reefs at Grand Cayman drop off from the 20 foot depth to 6,000 feet deep, making a great wall that all the diving buffs like to adhere to. The fish numbers are astronomical compared to other parts of the world. I guess all of the smarter northern fish head south to come here like the folks also do when the snow starts flying. The trip home was in great weather but when we were over Cuba I started having some instrument problems which seemed to worsen as the night progressed.

My first stop last night was in Tampa to clear Customs and Immigrations. The officer was a big, happy 35-year-old black man that was as cool as they get. He and the "Boss" at Wilmington, North Carolina are the best of the best inspectors in my book.

My second stop was in Atlanta's Peachtree DeKalb airport where I dropped off two of my six passengers. They thanked me over and over for such a great flying experience. One was a private pilot and the other had about ten hours as a student pilot.

Departing PDK for home, I had more problems with two of my five heading indicators, and when I completed the trip I had to 'down' the aircraft for maintenance. I felt badly doing so, as I had a Denver-to-Dallas-to-Houston-to-New Orleans-to-Huntsville-to-Home trip for today and tomorrow which my company had to 'farm out' to another air carrier.

Oh well, these things happen and I have to call the shots based on two simple questions—is it legal and is it safe ? If not, she sits until airworthy again. If it is, I'll fly her if I am comfortable with the issues and know she'll get fixed on the first available off day. I have a Minimum Equipment List that helps me with my decisions also. Anyway, anyone who wishes to see any photos of Paradise or Hell just give me a holler. I've been to both places lately.

I need to run some errands now as I have Florida and Bahama trips every day from Thursday until the 24th, then I'll be driving home on Christmas Eve for a couple of days off. Our Dispatch Board is filled with these types of trips like I have never seen before. It must have been one heck of a good year around here, I know it has been for me !

30.   Swiss Watch Night

Kathy and I were watching the Grammy awards at 8:30 Sunday night when the call arrived. Someone had died somewhere and was a liver donor, while someone else in Wilmington, Delaware was in need of that liver; but that recipient needed to be at the Medical College of Virginia no later than midnight.

This immediately was becoming a very time critical kind of Sunday night to say the least. I told dispatch I'd be out of my door in ten minutes and at the field in Schenectady in an hour. My first officer, A.J., lived much closer to the airport; he would take care of towing the jet out of the hanger, the preflight, and the refueling while I was on Interstate 90 inbound. I gave him orders as to the refueling and told him that I'd do the flight planning and weather briefing when I arrived. Little did I know, with all that was about to transpire, this night would end up ticking in such a fashion that it would equal or surpass the precision of even the finest Swiss watch the world had ever seen !

A.J. greeted me at the gate and grabbed my suitcase and flight bag and said everything would be ready on his end, and that I should take care of the planning and weather chores, just as we had agreed earlier. We talked over the fuel burns and weights again. Our nurse, Walker Useman, was also there ready to sail into the dark but clear northeast stratosphere. Ten minutes later found us starting engines with the outside supervision of Auggie, our local lineman and marshaller. The winds were from 310 at 7; I told A.J. to tell ground we'd prefer runway 22, and we were given that clearance.

As usual we were cleared to ILG via runway heading to 3,000 and then as filed. Because tonight's mission was so time critical, I had filed destination direct both from SCH to Wilmington and from Wilmington to Richmond International (RIC) airport. Most days on this sort of trip flying over NYC, Philly and DC one would never get a clearance direct, but tonight was going to be the exception! Forty minutes after applying take-off power we were taxiing off from Newcastle County's runway 19 and heading towards the southwestern side of the field to the Aero Taxi FBO (fixed base operator).   As I shut down the engines I could see our patient and his dad walking towards us. They needed us right now to come through for them. It was a big night for Larry and this was just the beginning. I introduced myself to both Larry and his dad and ran across the ramp and inside the FBO to check Richmond's weather and to use the rest room. Five minutes later we were taxing to runway 27 and again sped off into a very dark nighttime sky.

The complex clearance we had received on the ground turned real simple as we climbed through 14,000 feet. We were given radar vectors for traffic and shortly thereafter given direct Richmond and to climb and maintain 22,000 feet, and cross 25 miles north of RIC at and maintain one one (11,000 feet), Richmond altimeter three zero zero four. As I said earlier, tonight's flight could do no wrong; the winds at RIC were southerly at 9 knots and we were cleared straight in for runway 16. Just 27 minutes after take off we were taxiing onto Million Air's ramp to meet the awaiting ambulance on the western side of the field.

After a quick shutdown, Walker, our nurse, and I helped Larry walk from the plane over into the ambulance. He thanked me again and again for the best ride of his life. I wished him all the luck in the world. Then he and his dad sped away with the ambulance lights flashing and sirens blowing. I looked at my watch; it was 11:40; we had made the trip with 20 minutes to spare. I ordered a top-off of fuel, and as A.J. supervised the refueling I planned and filed the trip back home. The Swiss watch was still not missing a beat as 20 minutes later we departed RIC's runway 16, and 50 minutes later we shut the engines down for the night back home safe and sound at SCH.

I finished the paperwork and started driving home by 1:20 am. While driving I marveled at the outcome of the night—no delays, nothing but good things had happened tonight. The Center controllers had done their job. My team and I had done our jobs. My dispatchers had done their jobs, as well as the ambulance teams. Even Approach Controls and the Towers had asked us if we had needed any special assistance on this night. We had all done our jobs and, hopefully, with any luck and with the grace of God, Larry's transplant was a success and he is on the road to recovery.

Thank you, Lord, for including me in your plans. I am glad that I could help someone out tonight.

31. Day One At Flight Safety International

I should be studying but I need to tell my story about the first day at Wichita's Flight Safety International. We Captains go for a week of emergency and proficiency training—as well as all of twelve hours of classroom instruction—going over all of the Learjet's systems in detail.

Ground school was great as I have a new (to me) instructor named Bernie who has taught maintenance technicians as well as pilots in the Lear jet 20s, 30s and 50 series aircraft. He has taught for thirty-some years only in Learjets, so needless to say he knows his stuff thoroughly. However, what impresses the heck out of me is his unique teaching style: He says a thought or fact, and then there's only silence—enough for me to hear it, digest it, then understand or ask for clarification. I need this style. It always seemed, previously, that when I was trying to understand

Dana's grandfather, Grant W. Van Loan, in World War I. He trained for flying reconnaissance over enemy trenches in hot air balloons and biplanes, radioing to headquarters the observation of ememy movements. (*photo: unknown*)

Dana's father, Grant W. Van Loan, Jr., trained as a U.S. Navy fighter pilot in World War II. (*photo: unknown*)

Dana instructing Otis Moore on how to perform Lazy Eights and Chandelles for Otis' Commercial Pilot Rating. Dana taught Otis his ratings, from Private Pilot through Instrument Flight Instructor. (photo by Dana Van Loan)

Dana and Jason finishing paperwork after a trip is over. (*photo by DVL*)

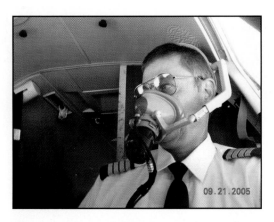

Captain Dana sipping oxygen at 45,000 feet. (*photo by Dana Van Loan*)

Captain Dana and Captain Ken Kamp in the Learjet. Ken taught Dana all his ratings, from Private Pilot rating in 1993, through all his Instructor ratings. (*photo by Dana Van Loan*)

Captain Dana and co-pilot, Charlie Albright, after a flight in the Learjet. (photo by DVL)

Tom Brokaw and Captain Dana, ready to depart Baton Rouge after visiting Hurricane Katrina's aftermath. (photo by DVL)

something that was just said, my teacher was one or two facts into the future while I was still trying to swallow the previous one. Thanks Bernie for your much better approach !

My simulator (sim) instructor is John, whom I've learned under before. I departed on Wichita's runway 01 Left with a forward visibility of a mere 600 feet. The first one I aborted prior to V 1 (take off decision speed) as I had master warning lights in my face.

The second take-off was OK as I climbed and turned to intercept an airway towards Hutchison; but, son-of-a-gun, I lost an engine soon thereafter and nursed the crippled plane into a holding pattern, shut her down, restarted her again, then climbed to 10,000 feet for my steep turns, stalls clean, flaps 20 degrees with gear down while in a 20 degree left hand bank, then a full flap gear down 20 degree right hand bank imminent stall with recoveries, losing minimal (less than 100 feet) altitude.

Unusual attitudes were next, with the first having me take the controls and opening mine eyes to discover us apparently inverted and accelerating out of control, so I pulled thrust to idle while leveling the wings as I then slowly raised the nose from 40 degrees down to level. Wow ! Next it was given to me in a nose-high 40 degrees with decreasing airspeed, so I rolled to a knife edge 90 degrees while slamming power to full while we waited patiently for the engines to spool up and get us flying again.

Soon I was holding again at an NDB, then flew an ILS to a landing. Break time followed and then it was my turn to be my partner's copilot. His name is Timothy, and we get along real well. He is a 26-year-old Captain and we're going to have a ball because we are both laid back, polite, and professional. We both know we cannot succeed without being upbeat and level headed while working in unison as a team. These guys will push you till you snap, so we have to have fun, keep a good attitude towards the pressures, and above all else—to learn; after all, they don't call this place the Wichita Flight Safety International Learjet Learning Center for nothing !

32. Day Two At FSI

OK, I'll admit it again, I should be studying feverishly but I need to tell someone about today's flying.

First off, I had several V-1 cuts and finally climbed normally to 41,000 feet where I demonstrated over-speed recovery techniques. The first time I recovered with power to idle and leveled my wings while at the same time I gingerly raised the nose back up to the horizon. I had accelerated from Mach 0.80 to 0.85 in a 60 degree bank while leaving the power at 795 degrees in order to get into this predicament.

On the second demo when I felt the onslaught of severe aileron buzzing as we were going supersonic I again pulled thrust to flight idle, leveled the wings, but then dropped the landing gear. This airplane will right itself, with practically no input from the idiot flying from the left seat, even though he just screwed up big time in order to get in this jam to start with !

Next, after all was again normal and in level flight at 39,000 feet, I heard an explosion and saw the cabin altitude climbing out of control. On went the oxygen masks, power to idle, spoilers up, gear down, dive at 265 IAS or Mach 0.83, whichever is lower. I had also disconnected the autopilot at the same time as I had reached for the spoiler switch. A Lear will descend from 45,000 feet to 12,000 in less than two-and-a-half minutes. You folks do the math.

Next, we flew several instrument approaches to minimums with missed approaches and holding, and dealt with many other in-flight emergencies. My biggest airplane handful of the day occurred while climbing out from Wichita, and around 2,000 feet above the ground I felt the nose yaw to the right. I immediately arrested the yaw with full left rudder but noticed my airspeed increasing at an unbelievable amount. I reduced lots of thrust as we blew through 250 knots and then I went to idle as we blew past 310 knots and we were still only 2,000 feet above the ground ! I told Timothy I kept accelerating out of control, and he finally said we had a runaway left engine. I reached up and pulled the left power lever to the idle cutoff position and instantly things were looking better. I noticed sweat running down my nose at this point, now that I was once again under complete control of this strange scenario. My two over-speed governors had failed, allowing the turbine to begin revving out of control. In this scenario the only cure is to cut the fuel from her or she will keep accelerating and then come unglued with the metal pieces probably cutting the plane into little bits as they shed.

Back to a controllable one-engine ride, I flew the ILS 01 Left to a 1,600 foot visual range (forward visibility of one quarter mile) and also departed again from the same

01 Left with a mere 600 foot forward visibility. I have only remembered a fraction of today's events but it's time to recharge. Tomorrow will be here soon !

33. Day Three at FSI

oday's flying found Tim and I sitting on a Memphis taxiway near runway 27 with a clearance to 5,000 feet for radar vectors back to MEM for a localizer 27 circle north of the field, for landing on 18 Right. Yep, the dreaded and dangerous circle-to-land at night while at circling minimums.

Outside air temp was a hot and sticky 100 degrees F. and we were heavy with fuel, having around 5,000 pounds of it. Acceleration was slow but steady and, exactly at V1, I heard a bang and felt the immediate effects of asymmetrical thrust. I lifted the pitch of my attitude to exactly fill my flight directors go-around mode bars on my ADI as full left rudder kept the longitudinal axis smiling. Under such conditions a Learjet 35 is actually lacking it's usual astonishing performance. I kept the pitch synched until knot-by-knot I saw a slight acceleration, which in turn I would trade for more pitch until at 400 feet above the ground I suddenly said to Timothy," Hey, Bud, lets DUMP FUEL NOW !!

Forward he tripped the guarded jettison switch and second by second things became better. Of course we were in the thick dark night overcast but by God a minute later found us at 1,500 feet and accelerating to 200 knots. Five minutes later found us 1,200 pounds lighter and leveling at our 5,000 foot cleared altitude.

Yes, of course we had declared an emergency; and yes, of course there'd be paperwork involved from the fuel dumping, but here we were back to a normal speed and a level flight attitude with almost everything in order once again—that is, if you can call single-engine Learjet flying "normal." These Flight Safety instructors actually drill into your head that:

Lear jets are really just single-engine airplanes with a spare!

Now it was time to see what the heck all of those flashing red lights were all about. We saw a low oil pressure light, low fuel pressure light, and a yellow generator light, all indicating a sick right engine. My scan was reinforced as I saw the a.c. electric fuel gauge also indicating a no-fuel flow to my right side, and then finally saw the N1, N2, and ITT gauges that all agreed we had lost the right engine. I talked everything over with Tim that we were seeing, then I reached up and slowly reduced the right thrust lever to idle with no changes in aircraft performance, so I continued the motion to the idle cut-off position.

Tim had the engine shut-down checklist handy by now; off came the generator and bleed air on that side, and open went the cross flow valve as we began pumping fuel, about 200 pounds of it, from the dead side to the noisy side. With this task done and the dead engine secured, we finished the 'after take-off' checklist and executed the approach checklist. Air traffic control gave me a vector as I told them I wanted to attempt a relight on the motor, and two minutes later we had them both back running, fuel balanced, rudder trim back to the neutral position and yaw damper engaged; then we set the upcoming instrument approach in the radios and briefed between the two of us. Believe me when I tell you there's never a minute that we are not extremely busy in the sim !

At the outer marker I was configured gear down, flaps 20 degrees and V-ref plus 20 knots, or 145 knots. Since we had to circle, flaps are limited to 20 degrees, and our circling category becomes C at D because our circling speed is above 140 knots. Anyway, we broke out of the clouds and into visual conditions right exactly at minimums as I turned right 20 degrees to get somewhat north of the field, but I had to keep the danged approach lights for 19 right in sight for the visual or else we'd have to go "missed approach." We skimmed in and out of the scud bottom but managed to keep the lights in sight and soon called flaps 40 as I started my final descent from 520 feet above the ground to the threshold. I chopped the power for my landing just as the tower screamed at me to **"go around, go around 200 Tango Whiskey, there's an airplane on the runway !!"**

Slam went the power as my right hand's thumb pushed the go-around button that is so nicely concealed in the end of the left thrust lever; its only job in life is to move the flight director bars 12 degrees above level in the case of a go-around.

As the engines spooled up, I once again buried the miniature airplane into the command bars as I also reached up to the flight director's command circuitry and pushed the heading mode button to give me runway heading. Up , up and away we climbed back into the overcast of the dark Memphis midnight sky. We were told by tower to again contact departure and they told us to expect the visual to

19 right. Did he just say VISUAL? I looked outside for a second to find us flying into severe clear conditions ! Man, how can the weather change from minimums to clear in the blink of an eye ? Oh yes, we're in the simulator, I forgot !

On downwind, northbound and abeam the numbers I called flaps 8 and heard Tim say "Ok...Uh oh..." I said, "Now what's wrong ?" Tim said he saw no flap indication and I said I felt none either through my control yoke.

We pulled out the checklist and checked the breaker which was fine. OK, I said, there's the culprit—we have no hydraulic pressure, so we have no gear, no flaps, no spoilers and furthermore we have no brakes. We declared an emergency and told ATC to get the emergency crews awaiting our arrival as we had multiple problems; I explained briefly to them so they'd have some idea as to what to expect . We were given holding instructions to the west of the field which we had to get set up and track to, enter and hold.

Tim and I held for a lap or two as we worked through our multiple problems. We blew the landing gear down with our emergency nitrogen bottle but could not muster any extra hydraulic oil from the blow down to use for extending our flaps, so we would be stopping with our emergency air working our brakes, and also we would be deploying our drag chute while landing with no flaps and at a speed of normal plus 30 knots.

Landing speeds and distances were figured as we came in for the approach and landing. Final approach speed was 160 knots and as the main wheels touched I quickly lowered the nose wheel to anchor us to the ground, and on my command Tim deployed the drag chute which we could feel jerk the plane as it filled with air. They say the chute creates a 7,000 pound force of drag at 150 knots ! I also was applying a steady force on my brakes with my hand-held emergency brake handle. I have to brake gingerly with the emergency air brake as I have no anti-skid capabilities this way, and blowing all four main tires would be a snap if I push too hard !

We were clearing 18 right after using 6,000 feet of runway to stop ! Another mission accomplished ! Next came several thrust reverser deployment and emergency stow procedures and many more NDBs, VORs, and still more ILS's.

If I could only record a complete four-hour session you wouldn't believe how much we get accomplished each day. But if I did so, I wouldn't have time at night for studying, so see ya later !

34. DAY FOUR AT FSI

Day 4 at Flight Safety here in Wichita was another full one. Ground school starts at 0800 and by 1030 Bernie had finished his lecturing and it was test time. Thirty-five questions from A-Z on Learjet 35 systems such as electrical, lighting, master warning systems, fuel, power plant, fire protection, pneumatics, ice and rain protection, air conditioning, pressurization, hydraulics, landing gear and brakes, flight controls, avionics and last but not least the supplemental oxygen and emergency drag chute systems. I need to know all these systems intimately, and their normal and abnormal operations as well as their limitations.

Weight and balance studies took a few hours this week also as there have been a few accidents lately that seem related to this topic. I figure these every day that I go to work, for each take-off and landing, but here I had to figure everything the old fashioned way—with pencil and paper. One formula needed for every center of gravity computation is so ridiculously complicated that I still can't believe no one has figured an easier way. Anyway, I missed a couple of questions but now know more than I ever have. With ground school of August 2003 now behind me, I can only say I have never met a man who knows these Learjets like Bernie knows them. He has taught pilots and maintenance technicians from all over the world for thirty-five years, meaning he was here teaching five years after the very first Lear 23 rolled off the assembly line, right here in the next door building on October 7th of 1963 ! My hat is tipped to you Bernie. I can only hope every Learjet pilot in this universe receives the honor of attending your classes.

After a forty-minute break for lunch I met Timothy and found my simulator instructor, John, in the briefing room to plan out the day's flying activities and to talk about recovery techniques for unusual flight occurrences. We've talked all week long about many unthinkable occurrences and they all sooner or later seem to happen here. There is not a more valuable item to have in a cockpit than a well-trained pilot or crew. Money alone can't buy this. It also takes time, experience and training from some of the world's best aeronautical instructors.

I flew several more instrument approaches with their respective missed approaches and holds. Suddenly, like a bolt out of nowhere, I flew through an invisible microburst which tried like hell to end my career as I was only around 200 feet above the trees when I flew into the beast. Power slammed to the wall, and hold that pitch high, even to the point of activating the stall warning system and all of its associated red flashing lights, and stick (control column) shaker, holding pitch attitude high so as not to be slammed into the ground by this invisible hand from above that with seemingly irresistible force was pushing us dangerously earthward.

Finally, as my speed (which had been Ref plus10 on the ILS until breaking out at 200 feet, but had then decreased in a split second to Ref minus 10) began to accelerate finally back to Ref, I called flaps 20 and started to see increasing performance by the nanosecond from that point on.

We accelerated, cleaned her up and climbed up to safety on the published miss and soon everything was well in this world once again—until wham ! Red lights blinding me and something pulled me forward out of my seat! The control yoke and column was literally being ripped from my hands and we were violently flying towards the ground from the clouds on a pitch black night. I pressed the master disconnect switch on the yoke as I pulled a 100 pound force to get the plane's attitude back to where it had been in level flight. I also reached up by instinct and flipped off the left and right stall warning switches as well as turning off the primary trim switch. The 80 plus pound force pushing me to my demise instantly disappeared, and I was once again settling down and leveling again at 3,000 feet. Shucks and Jeepers—that scared the crap out of me ! What the ? John remarked as to what a fine reaction and recovery I had executed.

For some unknown reason, probably a goose or swan or the likes had jammed into my stall warning vanes out on the plane's nose and the very system that is in place to save my bacon was actually trying to kill me. The system activated the stick pusher, which fires the elevator down, which in turns fires the nose down. In that split second we had lost 300 feet. I had done everything perfectly too. However, if we had been at 200 feet above the ground while on approach, I wouldn't be here telling you this story at all. You'd be reading some investigators' findings for the next few days in the newspapers for sure. I want to now steal a quote that my good friend Raymond Gould, the retired Eastern Airlines Captain, always likes to say: "I'd rather be lucky than good, cause good doesn't count if you're not lucky !" Amen to that Raymond !

Next I flew two GPS approaches into Wichita on my way back from Hutchison, and on my second missed approach, and while leveling outbound on the missed approach, I slowly noticed something wrong. In another second I felt the trim running away with an increasingly nose-heavy moment. I quickly depressed the master disconnect switch and ordered my copilot, Tim, to **turn the primary trim switch to off NOW** !

Things were not very good once again but they weren't getting any worse now either with that trim switch in the off position. I cautiously released the master switch and everything stayed the same; so then I reached down between us and flipped the trim selector to secondary trim and then started retrimming the plane to normal once again. Another crisis, another recovery. I almost feel like Morris the cat, but I seem to exceed nine lives every day in the sim.

We did much more than what I can now recall, but my eyes are burning from being tired out. Tomorrow morning at 0745 I'll be flying my official four-hour check ride, and this baby is the one that really counts, so good evening.

35. Day Five Check Ride FSI

Not just another day, but another BIG HIGH PRESSURE day finished, and no one is feeling lighter in mind than I do right now. I reported to ground school at 8 a.m. At 11:30, I took the written and got a 100 percent. I ran to the front desk to grab my catered turkey sandwich and wolfed it down just as Jim walked through the kitchen. After exchanging yet a few more flying stories, we were in the briefing room with the Part 135 air taxi oral in progress.

Jim flew C-130's and was Captain of a huge military jet airplane whose type I have forgotten. He flew in Vietnam, and at various times in his career he had been based in Guam, Alaska and all over in the States before retiring fifteen years ago; he has been a valuable asset to Flight Safety International ever since.

Though every six month visit here is stressful, I always seem to meet some of the most interesting and distinguished aviators this world has seen. This visit has been exceptional having shared ground school and lunches all week long with Pete Reynolds, the famous Learjet test pilot !

The oral went fine which included a few expanded discussions on topics such as clear and rime icing, timed approaches from a holding fix, as well as IFR departures from various airports. I have been very busy throughout this past year pushing a very sharp pencil as to second segment climb capabilities with and without anti-ice on, etc., so all of this fine tuning of flight planning seemed easy.

With all of this accomplished, we headed for the Learjet 35-A Simulator ser. no. 099. First I departed Wichita, ICT, with a 15,000 pound airplane and had two V1 cuts before climbing runway heading to 4,000 feet with radar vectors to 270 degrees to intercept Victor 75 that runs on up to Hutchinson (HUT). After intercepting and tracking, I was given a present heading vector for the ILS to runway 13 and at 100 feet AGL, with that beautiful runway in sight, Tower told me to go around as there was a fuel truck on the runway and to execute the published missed which is runway heading to 2,600 then right turn to the HUT VOR to hold.

Go-around from a landing configuration in a Lear is full thrust, pitch up 12 degrees, flaps to 20 degrees, at positive rate gear up, at Vee Ref plus 30 flaps up, then all of the 'after take-off' checks. Believe me things happen quickly on a miss, with two turns and a level-off and now how did you say we were going to enter that hold ? Is it a teardrop, direct or a parallel entry ? And now we were just nicely warming up !

After holding for two complete laps, departure control asked us if we'd like to come back around for a landing as they now had both good and bad news for us. The good news was that the weather was improving. The bad news was that our good old fuel truck friend had injured the ILS antenna and the only available approach was the NDB to the same runway 13.

"Fine," I said to Tim, my co-pilot, "we'll take it."

We were cleared direct to the NDB from our present position and don't forget, each and every time an approach is done we have to first do descent and approach check lists before we can even think of the approach. Wham! Red lights all over the cockpit and a swerve from side to side. I arrested the sudden yaw immediately and told Tim I would appreciate a half-scale of right rudder trim. I reached up to extinguish the bright master warnings as Tim helped to identify we were loosing oil pressure on our left engine and that he would find the check list for such. I remember saying it's a memory item as I identified and retarded that side's thrust lever with no change in flight characteristics, so back I pulled her to the idle cut off position and asked him for the securing and shut down engine checklist. I suggested to Tim that I would tell ATC of our present emergency and that I would hold at the NDB we were approaching so very quickly if we needed more time.

Tim finished the engine shut down checklist and soon thereafter we passed the station at 3,200 feet as I turned outbound on our teardrop entry for our course reversal. Flaps 8 were selected, and down I went to 2,900 feet, timing our one-minute outbound followed with a left turn to intercept the 132 degree course inbound, putting down flaps 20, gear down, and landing checks completed at this time.

"The course seems a little bit to our left," I said, and the winds at the surface were from 100 degrees at 10 knots which makes sense. I love things that make sense ! Tim agreed. We passed the beacon and descended to 2,200 and started our time. One minute and 40 seconds later with nada in sight I did another go around, this time it was a hand-and-legfull on the single power plant, and as Tim told tower Missed Approach, departure gave us a vector of a right turn to 150 and to climb to 6,000 feet.

Once level, cleaned up and on course, I performed a relight of that engine because the instructor behind me told me the oil pressure problem had mysteriously self-healed and soon we were back again to normal, flying a two-engine Learjet. Don't forget that we need to transfer fuel every 10 minutes or so from the quiet side to the noisy side to keep us laterally balanced. Now it was time for air work.

First were the stall series demonstrations. With the autopilot and flight director out of sight, I rolled into a 50 degree left turn at 250 knots and around for 360 degrees we flew, rolling out on exactly 150 degrees again (leading the rollout by 10 degrees) and then a 360 degree turn to the right to 150, rolling out as smooth as glass at exactly 250 knots. I honestly did not loose or gain more than 20 feet, and as the bank exceeds 30 degrees I add 2 percent thrust to each engine.

Rolling out, I decreased thrust by 2 percent and there you go. Power now to idle, spoilers up and trim like there's no tomorrow. The airspeed decays readily and we're still at exactly 6,000 feet, but now we're flying clean at a Vee Ref speed of 130 knots. I gently roll into a 30 degree left bank and reduce thrust by 10 percent, and wait as our speed falls below ref, minus 10, angle of attack indicators rising towards the yellow, then WHAM ! Red lights flashing all over the place as I slam the thrust levers to the wall and level my wings . Hold that nose up and be patient as the big fans spool up; here comes some speed, here is Ref again and now Ref + 30, powering back on the thrust levers as our speed approaches 180 knots again.

This time I am asked to configure to flaps 20 degrees and gear down, and then I do some slow flight at 130 knots and initiate a right turn as I reduce thrust by 10 degrees again. WHAM ! Red lights and a violent stick shaker again. I roll wings level as I again slam the power to the stops. Hold that baby up and be patient—here comes ref again, here is positive rate, gear up, plus 30 flaps up, and at 160 knots I reduce thrust again so as to demonstrate yet another stall in the landing configuration of flaps 40 degrees and gear down.

The go around from a stall and a missed approach differ slightly in a Learjet. From a stall we slam in full thrust and hold the nose high so as not to loose one inch of altitude, and we leave the flaps alone until we accelerate back up to Vee ref. The stall in this configuration happens at around 102 knots. As we pass V-ref flaps go to 20 and from this point on the procedure is the same as a go around. The difference is of course at the beginning of a stall we are flying 20 to 30 knots below Vee Ref.

Unusual attitudes were next. I buried my head in my lap as Jim leaned up and rocked and rolled my plane and then said OK, she's all yours. I looked up and saw a rapidly rising airspeed and a very nose-low attitude on the ADI (attitude directional indicator) so I rolled us until I had the blue part up and the brown part down and retarded the thrust as I slowly raised the pitch, and back we were at 6,000 feet heading 150 degrees still ! Jim had us diving earthward and inverted ! What a guy !

After bowing my head again, this time I looked up as the stall lights came on with the control column shaking and a 110 knot-and-decreasing indicated airspeed so I simply rolled until my wings were a knife edged 90 degrees to the earth and sky as I slammed the thrust levers to the stops yet again. Free falling with full thrust at 'knife edge 90' and

pulling absolutely no G's is so cool…you would never even
know it if you couldn't see…until the part when I am 20
degrees nose down and I level my wings and gradually pull
my nose to a level attitude, power back and guess what?
6,000 feet heading southeast!

"Now then," Air Traffic Control said over our radios,
"November 200 Tango Whiskey, you are cleared present
position to the Wichita VOR and expect the ILS 01 Left,
the weather is 150 feet overcast with surface reported 1,600
feet of visibility, temp is 12 degrees, dew point 11, altimeter
29.89."

"OK," I told Tim, "We would leave the landing and
recognition lights off until a second before touchdown as
with such limited visibility we'd be able to see the approach
lights better."(Don't forget all of this flying is at night!)
Around we came and in and down we slid—300 to go,
200, 150—oh, there's the lead-in lights, keep going, 100,
50, oh there's the runway lights. OK, I said, I'm outside
now, 20 feet to go, damper off, power off,
chirp…chirp…chirp, spoilers up, heavy braking…there…we're
stopped now.

Shut your eyes now and click your heels three times,
and here you are at Memphis International, on runway 36
Left. You are cleared for take off, maintain 3,000 feet and
fly the runway heading. Resetting and checking all of our
lists, away we went into the soup, for the Loc 27, circle
north for 18 Right (for you pilots just take out some paper
and pencil and draw this one). Established inbound on the
Localizer 27, 1,900 feet to the marker, descend to 920 which
puts you 520 feet above the ground and about 30 feet below
the clouds. We broke out to see runway 27, and at 2 miles
out I turn right to 300 degrees for about 10 seconds, then
roll back left to 280 degees and fly parallel to 27 until I am
just passing the lead in lights to 18 Left, then I say, "I am

leaving minimum descent altitude, flaps 40, landing checks," as I roll our baby into a 30 degree left bank to start our 90 degree turn from west to south, power back and trim down for a 700 foot per minute descent rate; everything's perfect now, perfect; I hit the bulls eye again.

Man, oh man, am I feeling nice. I taxi to the far end, run all of the checklists and take off northward once again, but mysteriously the clouds all disappear and here is a gorgeous evening over Memphis. I fly vectors around sight seeing and am cleared for the visual back to 36 left. OK, flaps 8; what's this, no rumbling? Oh, no flaps. Well, lets try the gear and see if this may be just a flap electrical problem; yep, gears down and locked, so tell the tower this will be a high speed approach and landing as we need to fly an approach speed of 160 knots right to the ground which I do.

I call for Tim to deploy the drag chute as I am extending the spoilers and standing on the brakes; as he does this he soon calls a speed of 80 knots and I tell him to jettison the chute and to run the after-landing check lists once again, which he does flawlessly. As I clear the active, Jim tells me to shut her down and that we should all take a ten-minute break.

As I climb out Jim shakes me on the shoulder and tells me I just flew a perfect check ride. Timothy doubles that motion, and as we head for the coffee break room this feeling is once again overcoming my soul from deep within me—this feeling that I share with the Almighty and myself after another amazing day flying the greatest airplane ever built, Bill Lear's incredible Learjet !

36. Owls, Deer and Sports Cars

Wow. I'm still tired. Am I getting older or what ? Highlights from yesterday's trip in one paragraph are: My best friend, Otis Moore, flew in from upstate New York with a couple of friends in Graham's Piper Arrow and had two job interviews with my company, JetDirect. I gave them a tour of the facilities and of my jet of the day, N156JS, just before Otis had his interviews.

Around noontime Pete and I blasted off for Jamestown, New York and picked up a very pleasant retired couple, whisking them on down to Vero Beach to their winter retreat. As I was helping them off the jet, Bonnie and Jack thanked us profusely and said in their 35 years of traveling this exact trip they never had such a smooth ride and had never done it in two hours flat as we had just done.

Pete and I then met a guy that he used to fly King Airs with and had lunch with him, his wife and their nine-year-old daughter. The dinner hour passed quickly and soon we were refueling and printing weather reports for the next two legs; the first was Vero to Morristown, New Jersey, and the second one was a deadhead back to Coatesville. At 8:30 our man showed, kissed and hugged his wife and daughter, and away we walked towards the plane as we discussed the Game—the Sox and the Yanks in game four of the playoffs. He was rooting for the Yanks and, of course, I was for the underdog Red Sox.

Ten minutes later we were climbing at 6,000 feet per minute in a right turn towards Orlando off Vero's runway 11 right. Thunderstorms were all around, and the lightning was so blinding to us. I kept slouched in my seat so as to block the bright white flashes with my glare shield, so I could see my flying instruments with the radar returns superimposed on all three of our attitude heading and reference system displays. I had to divert from course no less than four different times before we sailed on into clear skies. Just after cutting the corner somewhat near Orlando and heading direct to Craig (Jacksonville) and climbing through the low thirties we finally said the worst is now behind, and my job began to get easier every passing moment. Soon we were level at 43,000 feet and again cut another corner, this time the one from Craig to Charlie South (Charleston, S.C.) The moon rose quickly off to our east. Some day I need to study the moon and all of its associated phenomena. It literally seems to climb like a rocket and also can set like one, and yes I know it is us that's doing the maneuvering but it sure doesn't appear that way !

I asked an Atlanta Center controller what the score was as we passed over Georgia and he said 2 to 1 Boston, bottom of the fourth. I turned on my PA speaker and announced

the score; our passenger just nodded. As we approached
Nottingham which is just south of the D.C. area and is a
transition area on the Jakie One Arrival, Pete finally found
an AM radio station on our ADF radio and we listened to
Johnny Miller and Joe Morgan's broadcasting of the game.
How exciting does it get! I kept the ball game's volume
somewhat lower than Air Traffic Control in my headset.
On a very busy arrival into the NY area on a clear night
with your team winning, it just doesn't get any better.

I just wish I could have had my passenger listen to the
game too, but in this plane it was not possible to do so. In
the older Lears you could play AM radio stations on their
rear speakers. Nowadays it seems they listen to their own
CDs and watch DVDs on their portable players. Soon we
had to turn the game off as the arrival chores claimed all
our attention. From ten miles out I thought I could see the
rotating beacon at MMU but no runway. New York Center
had just informed us that the tower at Morristown had closed
three minutes earlier and that they had no idea of the winds
there as once the tower closes there is no ATIS or ASOS.
Weird place. All other Automatic Weather Observation
Services run 24/7. But not here.

At six miles out I had now slowed to 200 knots and was
turning somewhat to the east when I clicked my mike seven
times—and voila! A huge runway— heading 50 degrees
and a nicely lighted windsock.

OK Pete, flaps 20, gear down, landing checks please. I
re-clicked the mike three times to put the lights on low
intensity as I slowed to 140 and called for landing flaps. At
this time I also told Pete to cancel IFR with Center, and
about five seconds later I was in my landing flare when this
huge bird just missed Pete's windshield (and head!). We
touched down as another large bird again just missed Pete's
side. As I cleared runway 05, I noticed these nightly birds

flying here and there. I believe they were owls. And I know two of them were lucky owls, not too wise but lucky—and as my friend Raymond Gould always says he'd rather be lucky than good, 'cause good don't count when you're not lucky.

We deplaned and I ordered 75 gallons of jet fuel from my parking lineman. I called our dispatch to report to them our times for the flight, and then ran into the pilot's lounge area to watch the last three Yankees go down in defeat. The first two struck out and the third grounded out. Boston had tied the series at two games apiece. I was happy. Dog tired out but happy. Pete and I each brewed a fresh cup of coffee, he had regular and I had a breakfast brew. Many of the nicer FBOs now offer these little one-cup brewers where you can pick your favorite blend of coffee from maybe ten kinds, and simply place the little foil-sealed shot-cup of beans into the machine and place your cup underneath and in two minutes, presto—a fresh cup of hot coffee and a much needed lift at 11 p.m.

Next Peter called flight service for our clearance as I ran the numbers one more time. Soon we were holding short of runway 05, and as Pete called for our IFR release I reread our Morristown Five Departure Procedure. In this case it was fly the runway heading until 1,700 feet, then right turn to 160 degrees and level at 2,000 feet. On initial contact with NY approach our clearance was changed one more time, and 20 minutes later we cancelled IFR with Philly as we passed the outer marker inbound to Coatesville on the ILS 29.

Pete called our position on Unicom frequency and Dan the line guy replied to us that several planes had reported deer in the runway area; he said that they would make a high speed animal-clearing run ahead of us with a sports car owned by one of the line guys. I shook my head no as I heard this as we were still over 200 knots and closing in on the runway fast. I remember telling Pete he'd better tell them to hurry; ten seconds later I had configured for landing two miles out just as the little sports car entered our end of the runway and sped on down westbound. I told Pete that this wasn't going to work as I applied go-around thrust, pitched 20 degrees nose up , called flaps 20, gear up, then flaps up, go around checklist please. Soon I was 200 knots on a left downwind as the line man Dan kept apologizing for their blunder.

As I was reconfiguring the Great White for another landing I keyed up the mike and said, "Dan, what are you apologizing for, your runway run just saved our butts. I know there were some deer on the runway that were going to ruin our perfectly fine night ! Now relax Dan, and thanks for saving our butts !"

As I finished the paperwork Dan said the line guy had made the run with his Mazda sports car and had her up well over 100 mph trying to get away from my bright oncoming landing lights. I just shook my head back and forth with this huge grin…!

37. THE A TEAM

OK Dana we're at decision height and there's no runway in sight Charlie said quickly as we had just popped through the bottom of the low overcast layer that had plagued the Philadelphia area for almost a week. The flight conditions on this arrival and approach from Tampa had been nightmarish for us including a stiff east wind, heavy rain, stiff crosswind, wind shear and moderate turbulence from the final approach fix inbound to a mere 250 feet above terra firma, and here we were.

"No way," I replied to C. Dog as I slammed the thrust levers to the wall and then back an inch while tapping the go around flight director button on the inner core of the left thrust lever and pitched 20 degrees nose up back into the zero foot visibility environment that we had been into since the Washington, DC area.

"OK Dana straight ahead to 1,300 feet then a left turn back to Modena at 2,500 feet," Charlie said in a very business-like tone as he directed me through the published missed approach procedure.

"Flaps 20 and at positive rate gear up, and there's plus 30 so flaps up and after go around check list please," was my reply as I studied my instruments and leveled the ship on a southbound heading now given us by Philadelphia Approach Control. Charlie then told the woman controller that we wanted to try the approach again as she had failed to get us established soon enough on the first attempt.

"I didn't think that was going to work out too well for you," she replied in an apologetic tone of voice. She had been very busy working other planes and had us intercept the final approach course too close to the outer marker called Moses.

Next we turned easterly as I started reconfiguring my jet for another approach. First came 8 degrees of flaps at 180 knots, then as we turned left to north I called for flaps 20, gear down and landing checks which include spoilers up, flaps 20 degrees verified, landing gear down and locked, landing and recognition lights all on full bright, anti skid system on and operating, engine synchronization off , hydraulic pressure in the green arc, and engine air ignition switches on. These checks are always performed when I call for the landing checklist.

Next, Approach immediately told us to keep turning and to intercept the final approach course localizer and to track it inbound, maintain 2,400 until established, cleared for the approach and to cancel IFR on this frequency or on the ground as soon as practicable. At the 5 mile final approach fix I called for landing flaps and down we slid again through the turbulence from the nasty wind shears. I was again hand flying the approach as the autopilot just says 'no way José' in these conditions.

With the winds from 040 degrees at 18 knots our heading needed to point well to the right of our course to maintain the localizer, but this time I kept up with the glide slope perfectly as possible and right at 250 feet there was the threshold of runway 29 and the rest is history.

Our passengers had been briefed by C. Dog after the missed approach that we thought we could get in on the next try because Philly had blundered us onto the localizer at the marker on the first try. I don't think they understood what we were telling them but they were very happy we were home and thanked us three times at least before leaving in their awaiting Limo.

Charlie and I had to run through the pouring rain twice to and from the FBO as we cleaned out the jet and took our flight bags and paperwork into the office and cancelled our IFR flight plan on the telephone with Approach. Once done with the paperwork, we honestly thanked each other for working so well together on this day. I had helped him to Tampa as he had flown that leg of the trip and then he had helped me get back home safely. Teamwork with a capital T ....or the A Team as Charlie calls ourselves...

38. Cumulus Night

What a miserable flight home from Boston, starting at rotation from runway 22 Right. I knew from experience what to expect. I rotated the great white jet and at 200 feet turned on the engine anti-icing switches. At around 300 feet we were into the rainy soupy clouds when I started my left hand turn to a heading of 140 degrees. They like to send you (for noise abatement) out over the water while departing and making lots of noise. As I passed 180 degrees, departure told me to turn now right to 270 degrees. I reached up and spun my heading bug to 270 degrees and started to turn right. At this time the turbulence from the cumulus buildups and the wind shear was severe to say the least.

Jason said "Watch your bank angle !" I scanned all three attitude indicators in that split second and asked him what he meant, that I saw 15 degrees right bank on all three. My emergency attitude indicator was looking weird to me as I reached up and reset the quick erect knob.

The next Air Traffic Control transmission for us was to turn left now to heading 090 and to climb to and maintain flight level 210. I started my left turn and remember telling Jason my emergency attitude indicator still looked much different to me than it should. I reset it once again. The turbulence and icing was still severe as we were finally cleared to Sandy Point, a right turn of about 90 degrees. "Man this is crazy," I said, meaning all of these climbing turns. A man can get confused to say the least.

We were now through 18,000 feet and finally turning on course with Jason running the climb checks when I asked him what he meant a while ago when he had told me to watch my bank. He said he had meant to say watch my pitch attitude as he saw 30 degrees of nose-high pitch ! I told him under such turbulent conditions I climb and turn primarily using power, airspeed and angle of attack indicators. My airspeed had dropped from 250 to 220 knots while climbing out with a 30 degree nose-high attitude, but so what, we were in search of higher smoother air which, by the way, we never found until landing one-and-a-half hours later. We were getting lots of extra lift in those nasty cumulus now, and with a 6,000 foot per minute climb rate showing on our instantaneous vertical speed indicators, I finally pulled back some on the two thrust levers while trimming nose down. But while passing through 20,000 for 21,000 feet our climb rate stayed over 4,000 feet per minute with Mother Nature's free lifting phenomena, as Jason was once again calling "watch your climb, a thousand feet to go, now 500 to go, 200 to go, watch your climb man."

I was ready to roll into a left bank to stop this nonsense when all of a sudden the altimeter just stopped dead center on 21,000. Wow! Finally level and on course after five minutes of hell! The turbulence interferes so much with the airplane's pitot-static instruments that it's a whole new ballgame in these conditions. My normal control inputs and the plane's response to those inputs are so clouded with interference that every second I am wondering if anything is wrong with this or that, making it a very stressful scenario.

Then there was a flash of lightning on my side. Throughout the climb we were also scanning ahead with our radar for boomers and now we had a storm at our 10 o'clock and 20 miles, which other than the flashes and turbulence wouldn't be a factor for us.

Next we were cleared to our final altitude of 26,000 feet. Once level the ride was still horrendous. Some airliners were calling it moderate and occasionally severe. I agreed with them! Soon the noise on our two inch thick windscreen was deafening. "Sleet or freezing rain, Jase," I said.

"Man, what next," Jason answered.

I told Jase to request higher as my stomach muscles were getting sore from this workout. Much to my amazement, we were cleared to 35,000 feet. On this way-too-busy jet route from Boston to Philly 26,000 feet is always the limit, but the controller found a soft spot in his heart and up we climbed.

While passing through 29,000 feet Jason said he could see stars; I told him I saw nothing but instruments dancing in the turbulence. I scanned the outside air temperature gauge and read minus 20, so I turned off the engine and wing anti-ice. I turned on the wing inspection light and asked Jase if we had any ice. Sure thing, we had maybe a half-inch of rime ice on our wings but only out towards the tips. I knew we did because our radios were very scratchy and weak. Airframe icing means antenna icing too.Leveling at 350, the ride was still bad and after maybe five minutes the next controller made us descend to 20,000 once again. Back into the tops at 24,000 the ride deteriorated once again. More lightning. More turbulence. We hit a bump that sent my head into the ceiling as I retightened my five-way harness.

"This sucks, ask them for lower Jase."

We were given pilot's discretion to 14,000 and cleared direct to the Brigs intersection. At 35 miles out from Brigs I started a nice 2,000 foot per minute descent but the bumps just got worse. We passed Brigs and cut right about 60 degrees to Cedar Lake while contacting Philly Approach. Chester County's weather had been below landing minimums all day long with ceilings at 100 feet and visibilities from one-eighth to one-quarter of a mile in mist and fog. To our surprise the ceiling had risen to 250 feet with the visibility up to two miles.

We told Philly we had the weather at 40 N and requested vectors for the ILS to runway 29. I had planned on shooting the approach back home if it was at or above minimums; but when and if we missed we were going to Wilmington, Delaware which has a great ILS. I had even reserved a rental car there at Wilmington for my passenger to drive back home in, just as a precaution in case that situation developed.

I had Jason call our Unicom frequency at 40 N and request they "make a deer run," meaning one of the line guys takes a car and drives the length of our runway honking the horn so as to scare away any deer in the vicinity .

They replied, saying Ken had just landed coming in from California and that no deer had been seen. Cool! Ken got in, we may get in too!

Localizer was intercepted at ten miles out and at Moses, the outer marker, I had the great white fully configured for landing. The turbulence had finally disappeared! Over the marker I reduced power at glide slope intercept by 10 percent, and down we slid at 700 feet per minute as Jason called out: "500 to go, 300 to go, 100 to go, there's the runway, yep runway is in sight Captain, you can go visual now."

We greased her onto the tarmac so lightly that you couldn't feel the mains touch. We cleared the active as I thanked Jase four times at least for all of his help. He thanked me back each time also. It had truly been a night from hell as far as flying goes.

But it was all worth while when my sole passenger came forward and placed his hand on my shoulder and said, "Thank you, Dana and Jason, that was a wonderful job you guys did tonight !"

And you know what? There is nothing more satisfying in this business than appreciative passengers. Some just figure it's a cut-and-dried business and they expect things to go perfectly every time, after all they're paying all of this money out, right ? However, we have to deal with Mother Nature every day, and some days she just shouldn't be dealt with, but when we have to deal with her on these days, passenger appreciation is about the only thing that can cheerfully end an otherwise miserable flight. Thanks for the thanks !

39. New York City to Midway

Pete and I ventured into NYC at 8:30 pm last night to pick up our passenger, a fellow who was an author, and was going to Chicago to meet his publisher. We departed at 10:30 for Chicago's Midway airport (MDW). What a fabulous night for flying, with the stars and city light sights down below. But the high level turbulence was moderate to occasionally severe from Allentown, Pa., all the way to Midway. I was scared a few times, and slowed to 0.72 Mach for turbulent penetration speed.

An MD 80 reported severe turbulence around fifty miles east of Chicago on his descent and it surely was bad. Since my congestion will not allow my ears to pop, I flew out here at 34,000 feet which in the Lear means a cabin altitude of 3,000 feet. I cruised at Mach 0.81 until we started into the turbulence.

Pete and I were singing aloud some of the old songs like "Leader of the Pack," "Tell Laura I love her," and "Please Come to Boston," when I said to him, "Hey, buddy, how about getting me a cup of coffee and checking on our passenger?" as we were 150 miles out of MDW.

Just as he started to unfasten his belt, we hit a wall of turbulence as our Mach Stick Puller activated and over-speed horn sounded. I immediately reduced thrust to slow down, and the next fifteen minutes were scary. The puller activated twice more in the next thirty seconds as we requested a descent.

Cleared to 24,000 feet, I trimmed the nose pitch attitude down but the plane wouldn't respond. The turbulence was lifting us ! Pete quickly informed Air Traffic Control that we were in continuous moderate, and occasionally severe, turbulence and that we were unable to control our altitude. I learned long ago to let Air Traffic Control know of these situations and then they have to keep other airplanes away from us as nowadays we only have 1,000 feet of separation at altitude instead of 2,000 feet. This admittance should also alleviate any FAA enforcement taken against me for altitude deviations. It sort of takes the monkey off of our backs.

As soon as Pete had reported this our altitude rose from 34,000 to 34,300 even though I was adding 7 degrees nose-down attitude with thrust to idle ! Wow, I was sure hoping the wings would stay on, and it was such a clear, cloudless and beautiful night.   Finally I slowed to 0.71, and descending at 1,500 feet per minute things slowly improved; but at 24,000 feet and level we started getting hammered again in very uncomfortable fashion. We requested lower and finally out of 19,000 we found smooth air and the rest of the flight was great.

When we were level at 24,000 feet our passenger must have been really scared and started yelling something about the red lights on the wings. I believe he had looked out when we were getting beat up and saw our red rotating beacon light reflecting off of our tips, which I think he assumed the red glow meant an emergency ?

After our arrival and landing at Midway, Daniel explained to us as he was getting off the plane that he was absolutely terrified of flying and in that turbulence he had assumed we were fixing to die ! I apologized for the bumps, to which he slapped my back and said we had done such a great job because we were all standing here on the ground and alive ! He then said his publisher would be riding back to the Big Apple with us tomorrow night, and Dan soon disappeared into the frosty Chicago night.

I post-flighted my airplane with flashlight in hand making sure the wings and other things were still on and in airworthy condition. As I completed my walk-around check I marveled at what these planes can go through and about all of the engineering that goes into these jets that you really cannot see with the naked eye. I am always so glad to be in these marvelous Learjets when the going gets tough. They simply are way over-built and that's a good thought when the chips are down, your palms are sweating and you're scared !

40. Precision Flying

I left Downtown Mobile and picked my way between several thunderstorms which, down in that neck of the Gulf, are thick as fleas on a hound in July. They were scattered and not linear which was manageable for me.

Once aloft and level at flight level 410, we deviated around several more until well into North Carolina which was storm-free. The arrival into Washington, D.C.'s Dulles was with precision from 300 miles out:

"Learjet 200 Tango Whiskey say indicated Mach," to which we answered "0.80."

"OK 200 Tango Whiskey, do not exceed Mach 0.79 for now, descend now and maintain flight level 370 and you are cleared direct to Flat Rock for the Coate Four arrival." Next, as we were leveling at 370, Washington Center asked again for our indicated airspeed; I told them again it was 0.79.

"Roger that Tango Whiskey, descend now to flight level 290 and then pilot's discretion to 240; after passing 290 do not exceed 270 knots of indicated airspeed."

We repeated all of this new clearance back verbatim, and while approaching 30,000 feet, I realized I needed 2,500 feet per minute of descent to get to 240 in time, so I kept her descending. Normally when I have pilot's discretion, I will "keep her high" or as I call it "hang 'em high" so as to save fuel which now costs over 3 bucks a gallon.

As I descended through flight level 270, I was again told now to not exceed 290 knots which meant the spacing into IAD was now looking better and I could actually speed up another 20 knots which I did. All of this tweaking from still 300 nautical miles out from Dulles!

Soon I heard "Lear 200 Tango Whiskey turn one five (fifteen) degrees to the right for vectors for spacing." This is how an air traffic controller can fine tune the spacing between planes without making them adjust their airspeeds. If we have to zig-zag some, we will cover more ground and will increase our distance from the guy in front of us. In our case yesterday it was a Boeing 777.

Next I heard "200 Tango Whiskey now cleared direct to Falco, descend now and cross Falco at One Zero thousand and two hundred and fifty knots, Washington altimeter three zero zero one."

"Roger that, Tango Whiskey."

It's a fun thing for me to plan these kinds of descents with such precision. I try to figure everything to the minute so as to exactly cross a fix at an exact altitude and airspeed. This takes much attention to details as all of the math needs updating in my head every minute, since the winds aloft change, as does our altitude, with every second of time. I

control, I had satisfied my passengers and I certainly had satisfied myself. I also believe I had satisfied 200 Tango Whiskey. We sure were an unbeatable team today, weren't we ?

41. Almost Like Work

We finally left Tulsa at 1600, dodging many thunderstorms—even some tornadoes over Indiana. The Midwest was full of unrest—unstable air, with the clashing of warm and cold air masses, typical spring conditions in our country's heartland.

I landed in Teterboro (NYC) 2 hours and 22 minutes later after flying the ILS to runway 6 almost to minimums. After deplaning the three lawyers and ordering another 120 gallons of jet A, we blasted off runway 1 which has a departure procedure unlike most; and in a Lear one can become extremely busy.

The procedure was; "As soon as practical, turn right from 010 degrees to 040 degrees and climb to 1,500 feet. After 1,500 feet turn left direct to the Patterson NDB and climb to 2,000. After passing the beacon, climb to 3,000 feet direct to Solberg."

Those two turns after 1,500 feet are each around 90 degrees. With a fistful of take-off thrust, the flight controls certainly can become very heavy rather quickly, and the trim speed can hardly keep up with all of the forces on our flight controls. Simply put Teterboro is one crazy place to fly into and out from. Add in the overcast starting as soon as the gear is up and things can really heat up.

We sailed over towards Philly and intercepted the ILS to 29 at Chester County. Approach said a Lifeguard flight would be departing soon and we may need to abandon our approach. As we passed the outer marker I dropped the gear and lowered the flaps to 20 degrees, and Charlie Dog was extremely busy with his checklists. The glideslope (our vertical guidance course) was alive as I urged Charlie to ask Approach if we were actually cleared for the approach. He asked Approach just as the Lifeguard flight checked in, so the controller ordered us to go around, turn left to 180 degrees, and to climb to 2,400 feet once again. At this time we were probably around 1,800 feet. Up with the climb power and up with the gear while turning and climbing and then flaps up too after a few seconds of acceleration;back to 2,400, then up to 3,000, now continue the left turn to 270 degrees to rejoin the localizer, now descend to and maintain 2,400 and you are really cleared for the approach this time !

At the marker we slid down at over 1,000 feet per minute as opposed to the usual 700 because of the over 10 knot tail wind, as the winds are easterly and we're on the only ILS to 40 N to runway 29 which is basically west. One thousand feet to go; speeds good at ref (118 knots) plus 15; 500 to go to minimums and speed slowing to ref plus 5; 200 to go Dana; 100 to go; speed plus 15; you're at minimums Dana and I can't see—Go around—Oh, there's the lights! Continue Dana, I have the runway in sight now; 50 feet to go and ref plus 5—OK, look outside Dana."

I look out, see the runway and pull the power to idle as I flare slightly and plunk goes the mains followed with the spoilers immediately extending on my command, followed with extremely heavy braking by me as I lower the nose wheel to the tarmac

Charlie is almost in hysterics, and as we clear the runway as he praises me for such a well-flown approach to minimums. It seems lately Tango Whiskey's flight director works OK but the autopilot doesn't work too good below 1,000 feet or so, and I need to hand-fly the airplane following the director's commands. Anyway, as the gyro's were winding down this time, I was still shaking quite noticeably a good ten minutes later!

Ah, never a dull moment. We had flown half way across the continent, had seen several tornadoes and maybe thirty thunderstorms on this day while having to deviate course around at least five of them and had hand-flown two approaches to minimums as well as executing a missed approach inside the marker because of the Lifeguard medical airplane.

Gee whiz, if this pace keeps up it may some day seem like work!

42. Lifeguard Status Tonight

I was called the other afternoon for a medical emergency flight, just like the ones I used to do daily with Air Response. I hurried to the airport, and during the thirty-minute drive to 40 N, phoned in my fuel order of 420 gallons of Jet A with prist (an anti-icing additive that keeps the jet fuel flowing at minus 70 degree temperatures). Charlie also called me while I was enroute in the car and said he would be at the airport in twenty minutes, only about ten minutes behind me.

For the first time I can remember, the office girls had helped me—the picnic basket had been filled with thermos bottles of fresh hot coffee, snacks and condiments. I hustled through the preflight paperwork which consists of filling in the new flight manifest papers with airframe and engine numbers, hobbs meter times, weights and balances, as well as my flight plans and clearances.

Five minutes after arriving, I was trying to get into the plane which the line men had towed to the number one slip, which is maybe 100 feet from the terminal passenger exit. As the door would not budge, I set all of my armful of items onto the ramp and headed back to the terminal.

Charlie met me at the door. After shaking hands and firing grins at each other—as we both knew of the mountains of work that we had to accomplish in the next few hours with pinpoint accuracy—I told him the plane had locked us out; I asked him to run over to the maintenance hangar to get an entry key.

If you ever just shut the hatch on a Lear and walk away after a flight and forget—or don't bother—to run the door motor switch that lowers the door latching hooks, sooner or later you're going to lock yourself out. The only way back in is to find a key that works or to break in over the right wing by removing the emergency exit that comes out easily but is a son-of-a-gun to get back in place.

Charlie Dog returned with the key and we were over that obstacle. I preflighted the exterior and interior as he ran back in to receive our clearance and order our ground power cart, and also to fill an ice chest with bottled waters and sodas.

Our pick-up was in Northeast Philly (PNE), and consisted of five passengers: Three doctors, and two Organ Donor Company officials.

We blasted off of Coatesville's runway 29, climbing in a left hand turn to Modena, and as we leveled at 3,000 feet, were radar identified with Philly Departure Control as Lifeguard 157 Juliet Sierra (L 257 JS) and were cleared to PNE at that time direct.

Ten minutes later we landed on runway 24 and taxied to Atlantic Aviation's FBO. I shut down as Charlie Dog opened the hatch. Since no one there would talk to us while we were airborne, they had no clue as to what we wanted, so I informed a nice young man there that I needed a power cart and 200 gallons of fuel with negative prist; I also told him that we were a lifeguard flight with a planned departure time in twenty minutes. He nodded then ran to tell other workers there of their tasks at hand.

I programmed the flight plan that I had figured out while on my way to Chester County; with that in the box and 28 volts of DC power entering my plane through the rear receptacle, I jumped out to post-flight the plane with a walk-around, checking tires, rims, engines, fuel vent drain and my three navigation lights as darkness was fast approaching.

When the fuel truck arrived, I asked the driver and his helper if they were familiar with these new single-point pressure refueling systems that we have on our two new 31As; they said, "Yes, we sure are familiar with them."

With the fuel flowing, I kept checking the gauges inside the plane to assure all was flowing correctly and it was. I could not put enough fuel on at 40 N because of a 15,300 pound maximum landing weight restriction. This is always a consideration when a short hop is involved.

With the fueling completed, I went into the FBO and laid a charge card on the counter; I suggested in a gentlemanly way to the two working ladies there that no one would speak to us while we were inbound, and that it would be easier on all of us if they had been monitoring their frequency.

The older of the two ladies took my card and nodded to me to indicate that she understood my thoughts; as she passed the radio I saw her turn the volume knob up.

Sometimes, I know, when the FBO becomes overloaded with phone calls as well as radio calls, the first knob that gets turned down is the one for the radio volume; when it's turned down or off, a lot of times they forget and simply think nothing's going on, when in fact there is and they simply can't hear it.

Next I checked the weather on the WSI weather briefing computer; all looked well, with our destination Bristol, Tennessee (TRI) reporting winds from 240 degrees at 8 knots with unrestricted ceilings and visibilities.

After hitting the head quickly, I was finally ready to rock and roll. I fetched my fueling and GPU receipts just as the team of medics arrived.

Charlie was shutting the hatch, and at the same time he was briefing the doctors from Temple University and the Donor company's two employees. I began the starting checks and started number two engine.

As Charlie was hopping up front, I was starting engine number one. Within five minutes we were climbing westbound through the dark but clear starry heavens, on our way to retrieve from a car accident a brain-dead man's heart, to bring back so it could be installed into a dying recipient's chest; one human being was dead, but his heart would give a new lease on life to another human being.

Our lifeguard status was treated accordingly with priority, and we landed on Tri-Cities runway 23 an hour and ten minutes after leaving Northeast Philly. Except for the 75-knot direct head wind, the flight was clear and relatively smooth; the only weather that had been of concern to me starting just to the north of my right hand wing tip, affecting us only with occasionally light chop. There was some moderate rain in the 300-mile-diameter disturbance, with tops to 24,000 feet.

However it was nice that we were not involved with that. Half way there, and still being held at 35,000 feet, I soon found out that a Boeing triple 7 was just off of our right wing tip and was crossing our flight path ever so slightly from right to left. They were at FL390 and this was why I was held at 350. She was a beautiful sight to watch as our speeds seemed to be in sync. I wondered where they were going? Houston, Dallas, Fort Worth, Phoenix, or San Diego? Probably one of those, according to the angle of their flight.

Anyway, we flew straight in on runway 23, exited the runway and taxied to Tri-City Aviation. As I shut down, I noticed the brilliant flashing lights from the approaching ambulance.

Charlie let everyone deplane, and then our passengers sped away through the airport gate into the soothing, warm Tennessee night air. I sat there thinking that with all of this excitement going on, one living soul was about to loose the precious gift of life, but if everything went according to plan, two other lives were soon to be extended—our heart patient in Philadelphia and a liver recipient up in Buffalo, N.Y. That is a good exchange, I suppose, as the accident victim was still alive but brain dead. The two recipients were still alive but wouldn't be for long if this procedure didn't succeed.

As the planes gyros were still winding down, I sat there wondering, what constitutes a soul? Is it merely a brain? If we transplanted brains, would we also be transplanting a soul?

The next order of the evening was to order 400 more gallons of fuel without the anti-icing additive we call prist. The new Lear 31As have fuel heaters and do not require prist. The fuel at altitude tends to thicken in the minus 60 and 70 degree temperatures that we're flying in every day.

The Docs were to call me 45 minutes ahead of departure time so we could be ready. After a quick lunch Charlie took a nap. I chatted with the two pilots from Rochester that had flown down in a Beech jet 400 with a medical team to harvest the donor's liver (from the same accident victim) for its upcoming extended life in a new body.

We had a good chat about the War, the economy and the harshness of the past months' winter weather. They said Buffalo and Rochester always have brutal winters and that this one was just another one. Bob, who used to fly for the Majors out of La Guardia , kept bringing up the winter Christmas storm of 2001 when Buffalo had received over eight feet of snow in two days! He was a native from BUF and said that the airport rarely closes down— but that it had closed for two days in 2001. We also talked about the lake-effect snows, and how once the lakes freeze over those types of blizzards cease.

At 22:30 our team arrived. Charlie and I were ready. We blasted off with the same passenger load as we had on arrival—except for an ice chest filled with ice and a human heart. I also had catering for the medics on the way home as we had had on the first leg as these guys were on overtime.

Air Traffic Control was very cooperative, and before reaching our first PHL arrival fix to the south of Washington D.C. over Nottingham I was cleared direct to Terri which took us directly over DCs prohibited area.

"Cool beans," I told the Dog as we redirected the ship. There were to be none of the usual zigs and zags tonight. We flew tonight with Lifeguard status with a capital 'L' baby, so get out of our way. Soon we were cleared direct to PNE; we flew a straight shot there right over Philly International airport—ATC redirected all the airliners and others—so we flew straight as an arrow. I shot a left side visual to runway 24, and again the ambulance drew along side us as the engines were shut down.

The team thanked Charlie and I and quickly sped away into the night. I looked at Charlie and shook hands with him and thanked him for all of his help tonight. He smiled and thanked me also for our teamwork, which he immediately followed up with: Now get your butt in there and get me home and NOW! Seven minutes later we were done flying for the night.

Thank you, Lord, for giving me the ability to help out my fellow man tonight.

43. The Trance

I had not been too excited about much of anything lately until I pulled into the airport's driveway and parking lot this morning. I had been working hard for 24 days last month flying, when I finally got time off to go home to see my dear wife, but had only one measly day before she left on her Ireland spring vacation. Add to this burned-out scenario my dad's spine operation from last Thursday, my mom's hip operation coming next Monday, and yours truly turning fifty years old last Wednesday and, well, you get the picture.

Thank the Lord for Captain, my wild and crazy English Springer Spaniel, who had managed to make me laugh every day while home and had tried to snap me out of my much too serious trance. Actually, I think Cap made me laugh every hour of every day now that I recall it! I spent the week home with that great dog being less than five feet from me at any given time !

Anyway, getting back on course here, I was still in my trance as I pulled into the airport driveway for 40 N, but as I neared the lobby, I saw N 200 TW sitting across the tarmac waiting for me, and my big old heart just started beating wildly as I focused in on her. Wow! What a good looker. If there has ever been a hotter looking jet ever made then I sure have not seen one. Their lines and curves are simply gorgeous. Those jets were gorgeous forty years ago when they were first built, and they still are today. If I'm still around drooling over these jets in another forty years they will still be good looking then too !

After pre-flighting the plane, refueling, and completing all of my pre-flight paperwork, Keith and I blasted off from Coatesville all alone and flew down to Stuart, Florida to fetch our six passengers—three ladies and three baby girls. The weather was very hazy and I never saw the ground until, on our descent, I looked under the right tip tank and there was Cape Canaveral and the Shuttle Runway; man what a beautiful sight.

I rolled the plane to the right in about a 45 degree bank and snapped a quick digital picture. I checked the shot and guess what ? I snapped the shutter so quickly that the lens never had a chance to focus outside, but it took one heck of an image of our window ! Oh well, I fly over there all the time so there's always another opportunity for a photo.

Stuart was 80 degrees already by 10 a.m. and very humid. Once inside the FBO I sweet-talked the girl behind the desk who was collecting the big bucks into giving us a dollar off per gallon, and in those few seconds saved the company 300 bucks ! Voila !

At 11 a.m. our two moms, their mom, and their set of twin baby girls and a sister to them all showed up and we were turning money into noise by 11:20. Our flight path took us over Orlando, then over Craig, which is Jacksonville, as I saw many bad thunderstorms off to the west from Tallahassee to Savannah. Air Traffic Control was warning everyone that there were tornadoes embedded there. I was glad we were going north instead of west today! After Craig we flew over Beeno and Millie on up to Charlie South, and then over Flat Rock and Nottingham for the DuPont 4 Arrival into the Philadelphia area. Winds favored a landing to the east so I crossed the airport on a midfield left crosswind for Runway 11, and greased her onto home turf.

We then cleared the runway and taxiway, ran all of the checks, and shut her down. I opened the doors and hopped out quickly while the ladies and babies were stirring in the back. I trotted around and in front of the plane maybe ten paces to where the line man stood who had just parked me. He asked me what I was running for. I said I just had to hurry and get up here to see if the old jet looked as good this afternoon as she had looked to me this morning !

And she did ! Thanks so much, November 200 Tango Whiskey, for snapping me out of that trance !

44.   EARLY MORNING ISSUES

Five, four, three, two, one—and we don't have ignition. That was the way this morning went. I arrived raring to go with my work at 6 a.m. Paperwork first, then all the preflight preparations, fueling, clearances and then all other last minute details were completed. I finished the cockpit preflight checks and lastly entered the clearance into the KLN90B GPS black box. I hopped out of the cabin and closed the door behind as to not let in too much of the sub-freezing southern Pennsylvanian frosty morning air. I always do one last walk around just in case something surfaced since the real preflight, or just in case the other pilot had overlooked something—which would be a rarity.

The first shiny puddle of oil between the right landing gear tires caught my eye like I had been hit with a baseball bat ! Quickly examining it and seeing another drip to confirm it was a fresh deal, I told my SIC (second in command) that I was calling maintenance, and to tell the passengers when they were ready to just wait in the terminal until I knew all would be alright. I knew what was leaking as I have seen this before. Maintenance confirmed that we had a leaking brake puck, and that since this was one of the first cold mornings of the season I should go into my seat and continually pump the brakes. I did so but while doing this I felt the brakes feel very strange. I monitored the hydraulic gauge and every time I pressed the brake pedals down I could see the fluctuations in the gauge, which I had never seen before.

I told the SIC and my maintenance tech that I would not be flying this trip with this plane. I had noticed one of our 31s in the hangar last night when I had peeked inside to see and smell the new 1.8 million dollar airplane housed there. After awakening two dispatchers from sleep to see if I could steal this other jet, I then requested 156JS be pulled out from her sleep and to be topped off with Jet A and for the power cart to be moved to her. I told Razor, my copilot, to preflight our new ride and that I would go redo all the paperwork, refile the flight plan and fetch a new clearance.

"OK, sounds like a plan Viper," he said.

As I turned to go I spotted our two line guys, Brian and Ron, standing between the two planes so I hustled over and asked them if they would mind giving us a hand swapping the luggage. It goes better with help as all of the suitcases and other bags in a Lear must first pass up the air stairs, then through the cabin, over all of the seats and finally be stacked in the rear luggage compartment. The guys were glad to help and soon they had all the baggage removed from one jet and ready to be stowed in the other. With this chore done, I hustled the 1,000 feet to our new offices to redo all the paperwork and to refile the flight plan. Ten minutes later I hustled back to the jet only to find Ron, Brian and Razor Davis standing near the entrance door. They couldn't get in. Bill had gotten a key from maintenance because he thought someone had locked it, but still couldn't budge the thing. "Great," I said, "now here's a plane that we can fly but can't get into !" I felt the latch of the opening mechanism and saw the door seal partially sticking out of one side. "This sucker is just jammed, not locked," I told Bill. "Just hop up on that wing and crawl through the emergency exit," I said.

"Man," he said as he curled his upper lip.

"Go on," I said, "get going and crawl in through there and I'm sure you can put your shoulder into it and we'll be fine . He did all that, and soon we were stashing those sixteen bags inside once again for the second time in thirty minutes.

I preflighted the inside as Bill went to get our passengers. Soon we were on our way and I remember, as soon as I rotated, the crisp feel of the sleek new Learjet's control surfaces against the now 7:30 a.m. chilly air. "Wow !" I said.

Bill looked over at me and asked what was wrong. I said, "Nothing's wrong other than that I just love the feel of this bird this morning, Razor Man !"I should explain that we all have flying names for each other, and I named Billy 'Razor' on our very first flight together because he was so sharp. I have always been called 'Viper' because of the character in *Top Gun,* and due to the fact that most every copilot I fly with is young enough to be my own son. I am the 'old man' to them.

Philly Departure Control did their usual vectoring of us all over God's Creation until finally after climbing ten minutes and 32 thousand feet we were cleared on course to Binks. "Cool," I said, "finally we're heading the way we want." I never should have opened my mouth !

"Lear 156 Juliette Sierra, turn right to 300 degrees for avoidance of the new prohibited DC airspace, vectors for your climb, and climb to and maintain flight level 390," said the controller.

I told Bill I would try and never jinx us again by saying something dumb like what I had just said about finally flying towards our destination. He shrugged off that comment as he keyed up again and said, "Ah, Washington Center, Lear 156 JS can use all the short cuts we can get this morning as we're really behind the eight ball so far," to which the controller snapped, "Me too, and 156 JS turn left now to heading 120."

"What can you do ?" I said to Bill. "I have this job because I like to fly, and look, will you just look at all of this flying we're getting. We're an hour late and we can't fly south without flying northwest and then east, so let's just fly and enjoy !"

Son of a gun, within a couple of minutes Washington Center re-cleared us direct to Lynchburg for the Majic 9 arrival into Charlotte. I just looked at Bill while pinching my lips so as to not speak. I may as well have said anything I felt like at this point because within a minute that same controller asked me what my speed was, to which I said point eight one.

"Roger, six Juliette Sierra, do not exceed point 77 for spacing into Charlotte."

I remember grimacing as I reduced thrust to flight idle and watched our Learjet's speed decay to turbo prop speeds. The next guy kept us at 0.77, but the next made us slow to 250 knots the next fifty miles while we descended . I again should not have grimaced because the next guy asked for 230, the next for 210, until finally when at 12,000 feet and a mere twenty miles from port we were asked to speed up to 290,which felt darned good after this speed-limited trip.

I reached 290 in less than a minute, then was told to slow to 190 and to descend to 4,000 feet on a heading of 180 which put us on a right downwind for 36 Right. Spoilers did the trick as I slowed to 190 while descending quite rapidly at the same time.

"OK, November 156 Juliette Sierra, upon reaching 4,000 feet, slow to 170 and turn your right base; the traffic you are following is a US Airways Airbus at your one o'clock and three miles; you are following him. But your other traffic is another Airbus for the parallel, 36 Left, and he is at your 11 o clock and six miles; do not—repeat do not—go through your localizer; you are cleared for the visual approach to 36 Right and contact the tower now on 119.7."

"All of our traffic is in sight," Bill told him as we bade him a fine day. I flew a dot and a half above our glide slope to stay above the Airbus's wake turbulence, and just as he exited the runway, I pulled off my thrust and greased my five Goodyears onto 36 Right.

As I exited to the right on the high-speed Charlie taxiway, I looked back and saw the 757 that was behind us in his landing flare, and behind him I could see the lights of the next landing aircraft for our side of the field. It's amazing how these controllers pull off the spacing . I mean, with the vast mixes of aircraft types and speeds there seems to be one landing every other minute. The controllers are unbelievable, and even though we complain about off-course vectors and speed restrictions I really do know that they have us do what needs to be done for everyone's safety.

After shutting down and unloading people and bags, I couldn't half concentrate on my duties, as there were four F-14 Tomcats sitting on the ramp near us. I went inside to whiz and grab a cup of fresh hot coffee when I met the Navy guys. There were many of them, maybe twenty. I spoke with the four pilots. They had all been over to Iraq quite recently and had bombed the heck out of their targets. Last night they had flown down from Norfolk and had done two fly-bys over the NFL football game here. And this morning they were getting ready to fly back home. I couldn't believe how young the four pilots were. I don't think any one of them was over thirty-two years old. Amazing, I thought, to be thirty-two and have a Tomcat strapped between your legs ! I snapped some pics, thanked them for the risks they had obviously taken while abroad, then settled in on finishing my paperwork.

You know, when I had told my passengers of the delay and that we had to switch planes and all, I also told them that I would get them here safe and sound, and that was all that really mattered. They had all agreed with me and, as they left the plane here in CLT, had all either tapped my shoulder or shook my hand thanking me for all of my extra effort dealing with this morning's unusual issues and for the wonderful flight. They were happy. I was happy.

When I completed my paper work I was surprised that this seemingly slow trip totaled one hour plus eighteen minutes, whereas I had told them an hour plus fifteen. Not so bad, I chuckled to myself, considering we had the complete east coast tour from Philly all the way to the southern edge of North Carolina—and including getting two jets ready to fly this morning instead of one—and we were still only an hour behind schedule. Now that surely wasn't as bad of a morning as it had felt like earlier, was it ?

45.   NYC Arrival

Yesterday afternoon I departed Livingston, Montana, home of Yellowstone Air Service, after being there a few days fly fishing, hiking, and visiting with some of my many local friends who call this paradise home. I had three passengers: Tom and his two Labrador retreivers. I picked up my IFR clearance from Great Falls Flight Service Station on 122.2 while taxiing to runway 4. We were cleared on course to 15,000 feet and away we climbed into the blue sky and on course.

We entered visible moisture at 15,000 so on came the nacelle and wing heats. The nacelle heat keeps ice from forming anywhere on the leading edge of the engine inlets. Bleed air, hotter than 500 degrees, routed from the engines keeps the stainless steel nacelles warm enough to turn ice instantly into water which then goes through the engine along with all that air. Wing heat actually takes that same hot bleed air from the engine and routes it through tubes just behind the stainless steel wing and tail leading edges so as to keep them also toasty warm. One switch for each engine along with a single switch for both wings and the horizontal stabilizer.

We have disagreement lights for the engine nacelle anti-ice system. If I turn on the nacelle heat and the amber light on my panel stays on, then I know that side is not working and is probably going to build ice. This is not good, as ice can build and eventually a chunk could break off and go through the engine, possibly damaging it and even making it quit running. We have a colored gauge showing us the temperature of the wings and a separate gauge for the stabilizer temperature. If either one is not doing its job and is accumulating ice, we need to approach and land at faster airspeeds.

We flew into the blue yesterday at around 25,000 feet and enjoyed a ride in the sun at 41,000 feet for the next 600 miles, landing at Sioux Falls for a leg stretch and some fuel. Our two dog passengers (the Labradors) liked this fuel stop also.

Twenty minutes later we were enroute to Teterboro a thousand miles away, climbing again to 41,000 feet. The rides were smooth all evening, but upon entering the New York City area on our descent you could just feel the tensions grow as all of the inbound traffic started to merge with approach control. First I was given instructions to fly a left 360 as my final center controller couldn't get our hand-off to approach control; and by the time I had reversed my direction to the west I was given holding instructions to a fix I had passed twenty miles prior to where I was at this time.

I rolled out and headed west towards the Mugzy intersection which is on the Wilkes Barre Three Arrival into Teterboro. Bill told me when we arrived at Mugzy my new heading would be 335 degrees for our teardrop entry to the published holding pattern. Just as we were turning for the teardrop entry we were once again cleared back to Stillwater and were also told to plan on the VOR DME Alpha approach .

We were flying through moderate turbulence and icy clouds at 6,000 feet, using all of our anti-ice systems while all of this arrival maneuvering was taking place. The winds on the surface at TEB were howling from out of the northwest at 28 with gusts of over 40 knots. Of course the mechanical turbulence from these winds was rocking our ship quite noticeably. I had slowed from 250 knots to 200 while holding and now I accelerated once again to 250. Once I passed Stillwater and was flying a heading of 90 derees for the intercept of the final approach course of 125 degrees, I began slowing to arrive at 200 knots at ten miles from the airport. This is usually when I slow down, unless they ask me to slow down earlier than this or if they ask me to keep the speed up as much as practical until five miles out or something of the sort.

Our final approach needle came alive and the altitude step-downs started. First I descended to 3,000 at Wanes. Then I crossed Jaymo at 2,500 and at Clifo which is 4.8 DME from the airport I descended to 2,000; then I was told to descend to 1,500 and to contact Teterboro Tower on 119.5. We did and were told to cross the field at 1,500 and make left traffic for runway 24.

I knew 200 miles before getting here I would be landing with a 90 degree crosswind. As I turned left to a downwind, all of the Manhattan lights and skyline slipped past our right wing and I remember telling Billy, "It's show time buddy."

The whole cross-country flight this evening had been relaxing but now was the time to 'separate the men from the boys' as they say. I tried to fly a normal 700 foot per minute descent as we kept configuring the great jet for landing. I rolled out on a three-mile final and called for landing flaps, and soon I saw 20-knot airspeed fluctuations. Billy told me he would call out wind shear advisories for me as the ride and turbulence just got worse and worse with each passing second. The crosswind component was extreme and as I crossed the runway's end lights I wondered to myself if I had enough rudder to straighten this bird out of its crab.

We had hit our second extreme wind shear at around 200 feet and I was still flying Vee Ref plus 20, or 135 knots. As I saw the runway come up to meet us I reduced thrust to half, lowered the right wing and pressed in almost full left rudder. Lady luck must have liked what she saw and everything came together so very nicely during the next two seconds. First the right mains touched the runway, then the left main, then the nose as I turned in full right aileron, reduced power to idle, extended the spoilers and applied heavy braking.

As we slowed to taxi speed, I cleared runway 24 onto the Golf taxiway and remember thanking Billy for such a great job in helping me on this blustery New York evening. I also told him I was shaking. As we taxied up to Atlantic Aviation and shut down I noticed I was still shaking enough that I would not have been able to write anything readable on paper! I believe adrenalin causes this shaking as well as the inner desire to not be harmed. I think it's perfectly natural to shake as I did for maybe four minutes after clearing the runway. I don't believe I shook prior to landing although I know my hands perspired profusely while maneuvering for the landing.

I chuckled to myself as we helped our single passenger, Tom, and his two Labs deplane. I was thinking about how I used to shake after every flight as a new copilot back in the spring of 1999. Nowadays it takes an extremely hostile situation to get my adrenalin flowing. I also remember wondering if I could have pulled this textbook landing off two years ago or even one year ago? My friend Ray Gould always said that the only landing that really counts is the one that you're about to make! This one had been extremely hostile but ended well.

After discussing with Tom our next trip and saying our goodbys, we blasted off from runway 24 on the Teterboro Five Departure and headed for home at 8,000 feet. I told Billy I loved flying low past New York, Newark, and all of the New Jersey cities, as well as Philadelphia at night, enjoying the night time city lights. "As long as we don't run into a flock of geese," I also remember saying to him. "They could ruin a perfectly good evening as well as a perfectly good airplane."

But all was well with this remaining 25-minute flight. The winds were subsiding at Coatesville and were 20 gusting to 30 but right down the runway. Cool beans. A real no brainer.

"Lets do some paperwork and call it another satisfying day, OK Billy ?"

46. Into Pierre, South Dakota

All right, I admit it. I have not been writing about any of my experiences lately, and its not because I haven't had any worth writing about, its just a mood thing. Don't believe me ? Just ask my artist wife Kathy; she'll tell you that an artist has to be in the mood to paint a picture or forget it, you may as well do house work, lawn work, or walk the dog because your heart has to be into it for success.

The other day, inbound to Pierre, South Dakota with five pheasant hunters, Charlie and I were given clearance while descending out of 16,000 feet that we could descend to and maintain 4,500 feet, and we were cleared for the 14 DME (nautical miles to the center of the airport) arc for the ILS 31.

I looked over at the Man and he had a very funny look on his face that I find difficult to put into words. It was a

WARNING: CHART IS FOR ILLUSTRATION ONLY!!!
DO NOT USE THIS CHART FOR NAVIGATION

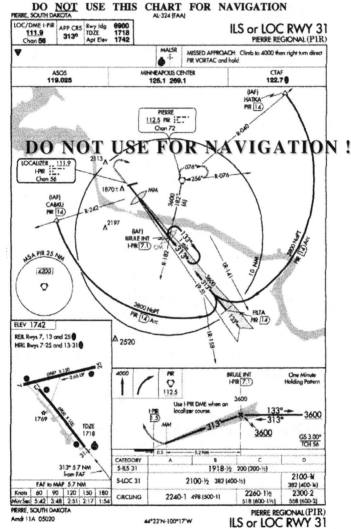

APPROACH CHART—PIERRE, SOUTH DAKOTA

combination grin and shock kind of a look; he was not ready for this clearance in this non-radar environment. His eyes were scanning the approach chart over and over again but they could not find the three magic letters he was looking for—I A F— our initial approach fix.

I said, "Let's first confirm from the approach plate that 4,500 feet is safe for obstacle clearance."

He rechecked the approach plate and confirmed it was indeed safe.

I then said that we would continue inbound towards the airport until we were two miles from the 14-mile arc (16 miles) then I would turn south 90 degrees and continue to try to fly a 14-mile arc around until we 'hit' the lead-in radial (LR 141). I would then turn right towards the airport and our localizer intercept heading would be 283 degrees, which would eventually intercept the final approach course of 313 by 30 degrees, which is a standard intercept angle. I cover two miles of real estate at approach speeds when I turn 90 degrees, so that is why I wanted to start my left turn at 16 miles out. The beauty of flying an arc to the final approach course is that we can intercept the arc wherever it is published on the chart. In this case, as long as we were entering the arc from between Hatka clockwise to Cabxu we were good to go. We actually intercepted the arc at about the 2:30 position if the Instrument Approach Chart were a clock.

I remember extending the spoilers to get down to 4,500 feet and to slow down to 180 knots approach speed, and as I arrived at the two mile buffer zone for the arc, I was still quite high, maybe descending through 8,000 at a descent rate of around 5,000 feet per minute. By the time I had turned to my southerly heading from my westerly heading I was right on my new allowable altitude of 3,800 feet and airspeed of 180 knots. And did I mention we were in a blizzard at this time with moderate to severe icing from freezing rain ?

Things were looking real nice though now as the Man called out my distance, air speed, and altitude. As the lead-in radial became 'alive' (LR 141) I called for flaps 8. We had left the localizer on my side of the panel and had to put the VOR lead-in radial on Charlie's side. As his needle was centering, I turned right as planned to 283 degrees and had him reset his horizontal situation indicator (HIS) also to the localizer frequency (of course he also identified that the frequency was correct with Morse Code as we always do) so we were now one big happy family once again.

We flew for maybe four miles looking for the intercept, and I remember adding in some more angle towards the west because there was some wind from that direction. I wanted that localizer (lateral guidance to the runway centerline) to center and I wanted it to do so at least three miles outside of BRULE the final approach fix. It finally came alive at around twelve miles from the airport. At ten miles out and fully established, I called flaps 20, gear down, landing checks please. Once we had gotten established at the ten-mile fix, I stepped down again to 3,600 feet and waited for the glide slope (vertical guidance to the end of the runway) which we connected with just outside the fan marker final approach fix BRULE which is 7.1 miles from where we wanted to land.

We still were flying through some freezing rain and sleet. I said to Charlie, "I hope this stuff ends before the runway becomes visible." My hot bleed air barely could keep the windshield clear of ice, so I had turned on our glycol which is an optional windscreen anti-ice system. At this moment I called for flaps full, landing checks confirmed done and for the Man to keep looking outside as I flew the jet by hand and 100 percent by the instruments until, around two miles out and maybe 600 feet above the prairie, I heard Charlie call "field in sight" at which time I stayed 'inside' with my eyes glued to the instruments another couple of seconds to assure we would not pop back into a lower cloud.

In another moment Charlie assured me I could go visual, so I went 'outside' with my eyes and made yet another greaser of a landing with my favorite of all the Lears, N 200 TW. I thank the Lord too that the freezing rain had also gone away when we flew out of the clouds and I could see alright to land. It was the first week of October and dusk had given way to darkness during this arrival.

This approach had taken maybe five minutes of intense concentration for both Charlie Dog and myself, but we had nailed the numbers once again. Like the old saying goes, a few exciting approach time minutes in poor weather puts an adrenalin-filled ending to an otherwise uneventful and somewhat boring three hour enroute phase of any trip.

I'm lucky though in a way because of where my home base is located. Flying into and out of Chester County Airport is always exciting and busy. It is situated in very busy airspace where the concept of a well-coordinated crew is always put to the test. I truly feel that I am the one that's blessed every day to be able to provide such a service to my fellow man and also to get to work with such great pilots. At this time of my life I'm wishing that it will never end.

47. 100 YEARS OF FLIGHT

L ast night's flight to Miami at 4 p.m. was cool. From 43,000 feet we enjoyed a much nicer evening of flying than we did the night before. The Philadelphia Eagles beat the Miami Dolphins. The game was awesome, the first half more so than the second. We left Miami's runway 09 Left and in twenty minutes were level at 43,000 feet, heading first over Orlando, then direct to Charlie South, then direct to Sea Isle which is on the southern tip of New Jersey.

This leg took us more than one hundred miles off shore for a while, and also took me directly over First Flight Airport on Kill Devil Hills, N.C. At exactly 3:15 a.m. we passed this historic spot. I was breathing 100 percent supplemental oxygen, because at night our bodies need lots more oxygen in order to see and think well. Don't forget that while I am cruising at 43,000 feet my cabin altitude is 6,000 feet. In other words it has the same density as the air would have if I were in Denver. Throw in this 'all nighter' for a guy who loves to get up 5:00 in the morning and get to bed by 10 p.m. and you can see why I am the oxygen man tonight.

Here I was more than eight miles high above the dunes where Orville and Wilbur made history in their Wright Flyer, and I'm here within a day of the one hundredth anniversary of this historic event. My mind raced while pondering how their machine has changed the world. They initially flew a couple of hundred feet, and in the next try flew for almost a minute. I'm sure they were excited of their accomplishments that day, but I'm also sure they had no idea of how the world would change forever because of them.

I was so comfortable in my toasty 74-degree all-glass cockpit along with my copilot, as were the six sleeping football fans behind me in the cabin. The air was smooth, the visibility over 200 miles. Sometimes in air this smooth you can't even tell you're moving, even though you're covering the ground at 600 miles per hour. It was certainly hard to believe that our OAT (outside air temperature) gauge read 75 degrees below zero! I had goose bumps all over me while I thought of how far we have developed air travel in 100 years. My neighbor, Jimmy, in New Holland, Pennsylvania is 92 years old. Man had only flown primitive machines for eight years before he was born. When Jim was ten he can remember hearing stories of flying machines. Jim is still here and so are all of the world's sleek state-of-the-art jets that are almost as amazing as Mother Nature herself.

And now I can really see that 100 years is not that long a time span. Actually it's exactly two times as long as I've been an air-breathing mammal. Add to my age now that same time again and you could have seen them fly from the dunes.

Hey, I'm still pretty young, right ? Well, at least I'm not old yet, am I ? People nowadays take all of this air travel business for granted. Heck, just last night I worked my butt off flying through some of the nastiest weather imaginable. I worked hard. Peter worked hard. My airplane worked hard too. She worked as hard as her crew did and after all of that work we accomplished one goal. And that was to deliver a small elderly man from Toronto to Charleston. We had weather issues but he just seemed to want to get going no matter what the weather was doing. I'll bet you he assumed the trip could be done safely even though the weather was atrocious. Hey, it's 2003 and man has flown for 100 years already, right ? There shouldn't be any problems after 100 years of this air travel thing, right ? We should have it all figured out by now, shouldn't we ?

Well, I'll answer this one. Yes, we have capabilities nowadays to fly and navigate through just about anything weather-wise. Heck, we even send airplanes into hurricanes to study them. Now that's crazy ! But really, with all of our high tech advances, I wish that unappreciative elderly man last night had looked at the weather and had planned to travel either the day before or the morning after from the time in which we did that trip. What is the sense of dealing with all of the turbulence, icing and instrument approaches executed without seeing visibly out the window until within 200 feet of the hard ground, while only being able to see forward three-quarters of a mile due to mist, fog and snow, even though flying slow we are still going 150 miles per hour ? Shucks, with all of that work and stress who would ever want to be a private airline jet Captain ?

Yep, last night's Miami-and-back trip was so much more enjoyable in good weather for us pilots and for my passengers too. And I really feel privileged to have flown

over those historic dunes exactly 100 years after mankind's
first flight. I bonded with the experience. I felt like some
greater being had set all of this football game nonsense up
just for me. This was an experience I will cherish forever.
For I am an important piece in this puzzle called air travel,
and I am so very proud to be a part of it !

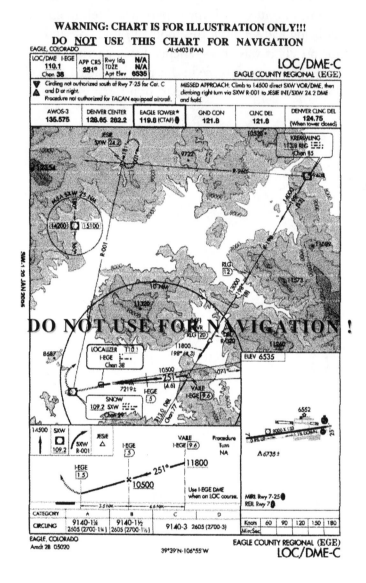

APPROACH CHART— EAGLE, COLORADO

48. The Wild Wild West

You know, when all of the action is happening there is no time to tell or write about it. This is true for both the flying and the work while back home in good old Fort Plain, New York. I have today off in between many busy days. I had fifteen days off in May, but I still ended up accumulating 60 hours in my logbook, which is a busy month.

I flew Saturday over to Bedford, Mass. and then to Aspen, Colorado via a Rochester, Minnesota fuel stop. The weather was 400 and 2 at RST, so the ILS to 13 worked fine. However, when we arrived within twenty minutes of Aspen I learned through Denver Radio that their weather had dropped to below minimums . I had already spoken to our passenger before departing RST that, if we had to divert, that Eagle was closest, then Rifle, and then Grand

Junction in that order. The problem this day was that a cold front was charging through Colorado from the southwest to the northeast, and the best alternate would have actually been Denver (DEN), Jeffco (BJC) or Centennial (APA), my old home base.

As we descended into the Rocky Mountain storms and associated turbulence I was very busy working the radar to avoid all of those storms, as well as planning for the approach at Eagle, which is one of the most dangerous approaches I have ever seen or done, second only to the Aspen approach. Sooner than I could imagine Denver Center had cleared us to the Kremmling VOR (RLG) for the LOC-DME-Charlie into the Eagle County Regional Airport. We were in some really intense icing conditions and I remember just about every item and consideration on the whole 31-mile-long instrument approach. We crossed RLG at 14,000 feet and tracked the 198 radial southward, and at twelve miles from it we descended from 14,000 to 13,000 feet.   Again at twenty miles from Kremmling we left 13,000 for 11,800 feet. At this time I quickly but very accurately dialed in the localizer to runway 25 into my side and set in the inbound course of 251 degrees while double and triple checking everything I would think, do and say. Talk about being focused ! At about four miles after this, the localizer came alive from left to right as we turned right to the inbound course heading of 251 degrees. At this time we were around nine miles from our destination's threshold and we were now allowed to descend yet one more time from 11,800 to 10,500 at the fix called VAILE.

Don't forget that with every navigation frequency change we need to identify by Morse Code its accuracy and at the same time we are talking with Air Traffic Control, also while out of radar contact with the world. In a non-radar environment if you read a step-down allowance wrong and fly into a mountain, no one will know or see you until after the crash ! In other words, son, you are on your own.

Of course, we were also configuring the great white jet for landing in these last three minutes while checking all of the approach and before-landing check list items. Still in solid cloud in an awfully intense snow storm, as we crossed the five-mile-out fix, we left 10,500 for 9,140 feet. Miraculously, at around 9,500 feet on our altimeter we descended into visual conditions and Billy called the airport in sight. I looked out and asked where, because I didn't see it.

He said, "Not out there, but down there !"

I looked 3,000 feet almost straight down in front of us and there she was ! I told the tower we needed a descending 360 in order to lose some altitude, to which he replied, "Roger that 200 Tango Whiskey, maintain visual conditions and descend on the south side of the airport; you are cleared to land."

A couple minutes later as the radios and gyros as well as Billy and I were unwinding, I remember shaking my head and grinning as I was thinking to myself we were definitely in the heart of the wild, wild west. I used to think that description was of the wild cowboys and gunfighters, but now I know it describes more accurately some of the most dangerous instrument approaches in the world ! Of course, now my passenger had to rent a car from Avis and drive the 90 miles to Aspen where I picked him up the next afternoon with the Lear. The weather conditions had caused this unavoidable drive for him but at least we were all safe and sound. Oh, and yes, he ended up pulling off his business meeting with no further problems.

49. To West Palm Beach

This morning's flight was fun. Just plain everything went nice and smooth. I arrived at 0600 and hammered through the paperwork. First I computed a weight-and- balance report and then printed out all of the day's weather, flight plans, notices to airmen, etc. By 0630 I drove from Hangar 4 the one-quarter mile to Hangar 1 where line service was just pushing N156JS into position. I loaded my bags and said good morning to the two line men, Brian and Ron. Pete my copilot had called me on my cell and was in our commissary doing all of his chores—loading refreshments, snacks, coffee, both regular and decaf, etc. Brian hooked up the ground power generator as I hopped in and closed the hatches so I could preflight the interior in silence, as Pete had already preflighted the exterior.

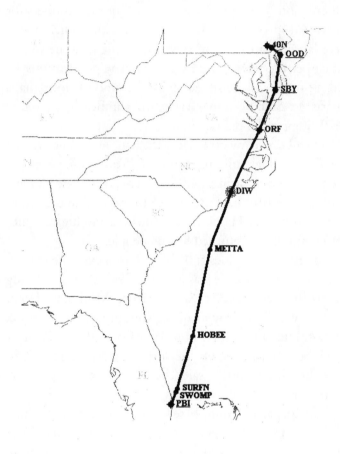

MAP OF ROUTE TO WEST PALM BEACH

I listened to Chester County's Automatic Weather Observation System so I could run all of my numbers for power and speeds for both departure and for a quick return for a landing, in the rare event such might be needed. I remember the temperature was zero, dew point minus 10 and altimeter 30 point 30. Next I found all four maps (charts) I would need to navigate to Palm Beach, as well as the PBI approach plates.

Then I drove my car back to the parking lot and walked into the terminal building. It was 0645 and inside were my five passengers awaiting me. They were early. Pete had just hung up the land line and had gotten our clearance from Philly Approach. He and I then loaded the luggage into 156JS and then I returned for the people.

I started the engines at 0654 and we sucked the gear up at 0701. The clearance was as I had filed: "Upon entering controlled airspace, cleared direct Modena, direct Woodstown, direct Haydo, direct Salisbury Jet 209, Norfolk Jet 174, Dixon Atlantic Route 14, Metta Atlantic Route 1 to Hobee intersection for the Surfn 7 arrival into the West Palm Beach Airport," said the Philadelphia Departure controller.

After departing home base I flew a 180 degree climbing left hand turn to Modena but before I ever got there I was cleared to 10,000 to Woodstown, then to Haydo, then to Salisbury, Md. Before I arrived to Woodstown I was cleared to the Dixon NDB (DIW) near Wilmington, North Carolina, and by the time I was over Salisbury, Md. I had been recleared all the way to Hobee intersection, which is out in the Atlantic from Vero.

I had filed the " shark" route from Wilmington to West Palm as it saves a few minutes from not following the coastal route. The water route takes us about 250 miles off shore,

with the furthest from land spot being adjacent to Savannah
and Brunswick, Georgia. I always carry ten life jackets, but
today I also had the twelve-man life raft. As I was briefing
my passengers before engine start as to the use of the jackets
and the raft, along with my usual flight briefing for a Learjet,
I recall they had looked at each other and then at me real
funny. I then explained to them that if we talked and thought
some about these emergency issues it wouldn't be such a
shock to us all if and when we actually had to use them.
Hey, I'm always ready but I hope I never need them.

The clearance next was to Surfn, and to cross Surfn at
8,000 and 250 knots. I did a steep but smooth 4,000-foot-
a-minute descent and soon I was hand-flying the 31 on the
ILS 29 Right all the way to 500 feet, when we broke out
into visual conditions with the runway perfectly in front of
us just as my instruments had said it would be. At one hour
and 59 minutes after we had taken off, I greased the great
white time machine back onto terra firma, landing on the
right main first, then left main, then nose wheel in the brisk
20 knot and 60 degree right cross wind. After a quick left
turn onto the Galaxy ramp followed by a three-second shut
down, all became quiet again as I hopped out of my seat to
open the hatch.

I commented to my passenger, Bob, that everything so
far had gone perfectly. He said he couldn't believe it was
only a two hour flight to southern Florida as it is always
more like two point three hours. I smiled back at him and
said, "Correction, almost always, but not today." I had
initially climbed to 43,000 and had stepped to 45,000 over
North Carolina. Our normal headwinds were crosswinds,
and other traffic was sparse.

Many reasons made this morning's flight a real pleasant
experience. After all, the training which I had taken at Flight
Safety International last week in Wichita would make

almost any flight a pleasant experience ! Do you think I owe those Wichita Learning Center instructors yet another Thank You for all of my training ?

50. Maintenance Check-ride With Bill

My good friend Bill is a very hard working receptionist at Jet Direct Aviation. He is also very crippled and confined to a wheelchair for life . He was a young aspiring flight instructor at Chester County Airport with 1,200 hours, building time for a someday job as a professional pilot flying jets when he became stricken with a multitude of bad things and diseases which nearly took his life. Not being one to ever throw in the towel, he fought back through several transplants and other operations and now is the main man behind the counter at our operations terminal . His hands are also crippled shut, but nothing will stop William from living his life near the airplanes he so deeply loves.

I was doing some last minute Christmas shopping today and swung by the airport to do some final paperwork for the records I had from the last flight, and also to further check out the details of my upcoming trips to Florida and the Bahamas . I was about to leave the building when my name came over the PA system to call the Director of Operations, Troy, who is also another good friend. I called him to ask what was up. He said the mechanics thought they had the problem solved in Tango Whiskey and wondered if I could fly a test flight to confirm it was fixed.

I said sure, I'd be ready in a couple of minutes. As I hung up the phone I turned to Bill and said, "Here's your chance at last for your dream ride in the Lear. His eyes grew huge immediately but he then quickly reminded me that he was working and that he probably couldn't go. So then I trotted into the next office to see the airport's Supervisor, named Bruce. He said Bill could go and that he would cover for him. Cool beans.

Bill, Troy and I were soon inside the sealed fuselage running the checks. It was a clear day here and I told Troy we would go VFR westbound at 4,500 feet. Our take-off weight was a light 13,000 pounds and I knew Bill was about to experience the ride of his life. Believe me, there's not too many things mechanical on this earth that are more impressive performance-wise than a very lightly loaded Learjet. Troy asked if he could be the pilot flying as he hardly gets to fly anymore as his job as D.O. (director of operations) keeps him somewhat ground-bound. At Vr (rotation speed) we rotated 30 some degrees upward and before you could blink twice I had the gear up, yaw damper on, flaps up and all of the after-take-off checks done. I could hear Bill howling and yelling like a little kid with a grin a mile-and-three quarters wide ! We cleared to the west and halfway to Lancaster we did steep turns both to the left and right at around 250 knots while accelerating and decelerating, performing our checks for the maintenance technicians. Everything on the instruments suited me just fine at this point, so I called the tower at Lancaster from fifteen miles south and requested to circle the airport and then we'd depart to the east. I also told Tower that we were on a check ride. Tower said to call again from five miles out; when I did he asked me if I would be willing to fly a low pass in front of them using runway 26. I replied, "Sure, we'd love to entertain y'all !"

He asked me to fly a three-mile left downwind to 26 and they would have the cameras rolling when we came by. A minute later, we were five feet above the deck all cleaned up, and at 200 knots the runway's end was fast approaching. After passing the Tower we pulled her up to about 40 degrees and added in lots of thrust as our Instantaneous Vertical Speed Indicator pegged at its gauge limit of 10 thousand feet per minute ascent ! Once again the cabin filled with shrieks and moans of joy from Bill as he was howling for all he was worth. I'll bet they probably heard him from the Tower !

We flew on back to home base and this maintenance check ride was complete. The plane had been fixed and tested once again, but the real satisfaction for me on this day I pondered as I was loading Bill back into his wheelchair was that I had really made his day. I had given him a few minutes that he will never forget for as long as he lives. Thank you, William, for giving me the pleasure of giving you that ride !

51. Night Time Turbulence

I rested for a mid-afternoon hour, since Pete and I would be flying from the beginning of evening well into the wee small hours. We left Coatesville and headed into the Big Apple to pick up our passenger and then fly him to Montana. It's Thursday, nine eleven, two thousand and three. He was on time to the exact minute after having had to work his job until 19:00. At 20:15 local time I was rotating N156JS skyward off of TEB s runway 01 with clearance for the Teterboro 5 departure procedure, then direct Coate, Lake Henry, Stoney Fork, Badger, and finally to Sioux Falls, S.D. where I wanted to take a twenty-minute break and refuel.

The TEB 5 calls for a right turn to 40 degrees as soon as practical until reaching 1,500 feet, then a left turn direct Patterson Non-Directional Beacon while climbing to 2,000 feet; and after passing the beacon climb to and maintain 3,000 feet. With this all behind me and now into my second minute of flight, we were given vectors for traffic avoidance and soon told to fly direct Coate and to resume our own navigation.

Things were very routine until, as we were climbing through the low thirties, we encountered very moderate turbulence. I noticed my flight director telling the automatic flight control system to steer left; my eyes were scanning this scenario in high gear using many bytes of gray matter. I finally saw the culprit that was upsetting my crew and my passenger—we were flying into a very powerful jet stream that came from the eastern Tennessee area and was flowing northward towards Montreal. We had had no winds aloft at all to speak of up until this point and now I had 140 knots of cross wind ! Simply amazing that we had flown into this invisible raging river of air. No wonder we were getting hammered ! Once well inside the flowing mass, things became more comfortable again on this now 9:30 p.m. evening—that is until we crossed a major cold front that split the continent in half; the contour of the front just about following the shape of our Mississippi River from northern Minnesota all the way south to Dallas !

As we crossed the border into Iowa things were moving around again inside the plane. I asked for any ride reports ahead and the controller said no altitudes were smooth. I had initially climbed to 43,000 feet and as I was mostly topping all of this system's clouds, scud and convective activity, I wasn't about to change altitudes if I could help it. The ride was irritatingly choppy but that was the best I could do. At 120 miles out from our destination, I pulled the thrust levers to idle and set up a 3,000 foot per minute descent into Joe Foss Field.

We had cleared the cold front, and as we neared FSD the clouds kept thinning until out of ten thousand feet we saw the city, then the beacon, then the approach lights, then the runway. I greased her onto runway 21, and moments later as I shut down the engines, Business Aviation line guys had the GPU (ground power unit) hooked up to our plane, and fuel pumping. Pete fetched the clearance while I did my usual walk-around after-landing inspection checking tires, wheels, fuel vent drains, engines and wings to make sure everything was alright and still attached Especially so after that turbulence!

My passenger was inside reading the local paper as this was his hometown. I came in and he and I both checked the weather for the remainder of our flight. There was another cold front to pass but this one seemed much smaller and looked as if it would be much quieter to deal with, or so I thought.

Twenty minutes after silencing the big Garretts I was once again turning money into noise. We departed runway 33 and with a slight left hand turn were direct Pierre. As we climbed we once again saw the winds aloft from 50 degrees to our left coming from over towards the Phoenix area. Soon we leveled at 39,000 feet and had a very choppy ride. I asked for 41,000 feet and soon we leveled at flight level 410. Still rougher than a cob.

I asked for any ride reports up ahead, and Denver Center said no smooth altitudes above 31,000 feet. With the 110 knot headwinds we saw while climbing through the low 30s, I was certainly not ready to descend. But all of this theory was soon to be amended.

Wham ! Wham ! Boom ! Wham ! Then wham again ! I disengaged all automatic flight control systems as I keyed the mike with my left pointer finger and hollered to Denver,

"November156 Juliet Sierra is in severe turbulence, requesting an immediate descent." It felt like we had flown into a granite wall, or maybe Hell for that matter.

"Roger 6 Juliet Sierra, it will be a minute or two; OK Juliet Sierra, descend now and maintain flight level 300."

When he first had said a couple of minutes, I was all ready to tell him no, we're going to descend now, but he had quickly reacted to my call and in a split second had given me what I had wanted. Of course, when I had disengaged the autopilot I had also turned on the igniters so we would keep the Garretts whining. In severe turbulence it would not be surprising to experience a compressor stall; then the engines could flame out as a result of air going backwards through the turbines. Or more precisely, the amount of air going through the inlet would be so radically altered that the turbines' inner core could stop burning fuel which of course would not be a good thing! But these things can and do happen, so get your sparkers sparking just like on your gas grill on a windy day!

When in severe turbulence an aircraft is pretty much doing whatever it wants to do. I can only attempt to keep it right side up. Altitude changes by the mini-second in these violent updrafts and downdrafts, and any attempt to maintain altitude could over stress the airframe. One cannot read the instruments when things are moving wildly like this. If I had held my hand up in front of my copilot's face with say three fingers showing and asked him how many he saw, he wouldn't have a clue; the eyes cannot focus rapidly in such chaotic conditions. That's how I judge severe turbulence!

As we passed 37,000 feet the ride became smoother and smoother until I reported to an anxiously awaiting Air Traffic Control guy that the severe had ended at 39,000 feet. He would relay this information   so that no one else would have to experience this sticky situation. I flew the length of Montana at FL300; at 75 miles out from Bozeman I pulled the thrust to almost flight idle and I had all of my anti-icing equipment on as the ice-laden clouds were 12,000 feet thick and bumpier than the dickens !

We topped the 12,000-foot-high snow covered peaks on the ridge that I was painting on radar and finally flew into visual conditions just as I passed the airport. I told Pete to cancel IFR, and then I hit the spoilers while S turning and flying a 180, entering a right downwind for 30. Bozeman Tower cleared us for landing as we were midfield and I again greased her onto terra firma.

After shutting down I told my passenger friend that we had experienced some unreported severe turbulence to which he replied with a huge grin, "No kidding, Dana !"

As I opened the hatch I was thinking maybe I had said that the wrong way? Nah, he was only ribbing me. He knows that I give my best on every flight. Hey, it was just one of those nights. We had been beaten up across the entire girth of this nation, but here we were safe and sound and another day wiser. 09-11-03 was an hour away from being history, mountain time. Now it was time to unwind for the night. Some days are just harder than others. You just have to make do the best you can.

52. Shark vs. Land Routes

My filed flight plan for today from West Palm Beach to Chester County is again over the Shark Route— pilots' jargon for over-water routing . The straighter Shark Route saves perhaps sixty miles, which mathematically figures out to a five-minute savings; monetarily this figures out to a $165 fuel savings over the land route which more-or-less follows the contour of the East Coast.

However, when you figure out the savings gained from this much less congested airspace with it's associated less vectoring, ease of climbing higher as the trip progresses to save fuel (since the Shark route is the road less traveled) the savings keep mounting. The land route today would have us flying northwest-ward for the length of Florida; this would certainly slow our planned 460 knot ground speed somewhat due to the head wind component at altitude from the Jet Stream.

Flying more northerly over the Shark Route eliminates the head wind component by quite a bit for the first hour, so I'm figuring in an extra three minutes of saved time at the very least; that brings up our total time saved to eight minutes, with the money-saved figure coming in at $264.

But there is still more. Since the land route is so much more congested than the water route, we usually can expect to get additional vectors from Air Traffic Control; this on an average could add up to yet another couple of minutes. Usually all the jets departing from Miami, Fort Lauderdale and West Palm Beach are funneled over Orlando, as this is the preferred departure path north-bound for kerosene burning airplanes. We can expect vectors here for spacing, not to mention being held down in the lower altitudes— also due to this winter time traffic saturation issue. Add in yet again all of the Orlando departures and you'll get to see the picture from a pilot's perspective: Clustering.

The next area where congestion usually starts is about 120 miles south of Norfolk, near the Wilmington, North Carolina area; this is where the second or third Washington Center controller whom we contact on our northbound trek will start spacing us for arrivals into the DC, Philly and NY areas. It is very common while flying the northward land arrival for pilots to be given the clearance to "cross 80 miles south of Norfolk, at and maintain flight level 290" (29,000 feet). This almost always makes me grimace, and sometimes I query the controller, "Confirm we are landing 40N, or PHL or TEB", whichever is the case.

I'm grimacing because the issue here in descending while still so far away from your destination is fuel burn: While at 45,000 feet we may see a total fuel burn per hour of 900 pounds; descending into the twenties we will see more like 1600 pounds per hour.

The controller usually comes back with "Affirmative Lear 6 Juliet Sierra; this is the next sector's request for spacing into the (whatever) area."

And don't forget all of the airspeed restrictions which are common, starting in the Norfolk area when things get busy, especially on a Sunday evening during rush hour. These land route problems can easily add yet another couple of minutes to our totals, so we finally end up with the Shark Route saving us possibly twelve minutes and $400. Of course, none of this is possible if there's considerable weather over the water route or if my passengers happen to request not flying over the water, which some happen to do on occasion. Also the ride is usually smoother over the water route due to less thermal activity from below. And lastly, arrivals from the Shark Route usually get to stay at the lofty altitudes for a much longer time due to being east and away from the clustered traffic. This all sounds good and fine, but the numbers will really tell the story this evening at 18;30 local hours when I finish up my paperwork.

Oh, and there's yet one more thought. Whenever I pick one route over the other and actually complete the trip, I always have the facts and figures from that trip, but of course I don't have any information on what the actual numbers would have been from the alternate route, had we taken it. That's why us guys get paid the "big bucks" as they say, to make those big decisions!

53. Man and Machine

I slept so soundly last night that when I came to this morning the blankets had not been rustled one bit! We departed Orlando on time at 14:30 for our two hour and ten minute flight to Coatesville, Pennsylvania. This afternoon, First Officer Charles W. Albright was the pilot flying and Captain Dana L. Van Loan was the pilot not flying.

The climb out was smooth and scenic as we climbed for twenty minutes into the clear heavens while watching the stretches of Florida's white sands below lengthen into hundreds of miles of shorelines. I always figured on a clear day we can see about 220 miles. Our departure clearance was radar vectors to Craig (Jacksonville) then direct Savannah, direct Charlie South, direct Flat Rock for our DuPont 4 arrival into the Philadelphia area.

Security is very intense these days; I can feel it more so while flying these busy east coast routes. All was well and normal until my radio sounded scratchy. I asked Center for a radio check for 200 Tango Whiskey, but my request got no reply. We were fast approaching FAK, and since I often fly this route, I knew Washington Center likes to have us cross this fix in the 20s. I heard a Navy fighter sign in and I asked him for a radio check but the result was the same— no answer.

I quickly called Leesburg Flight Service on the generic 122.2 frequency and told him of my lost radio contact situation as well as my location and altitude. He gave me a Washington Center Frequency; when I tried that, the controller shot back at me, " 200 Tango Whiskey, where have you been ? We've been trying to talk to you for 180 miles !"

My mouth must have dropped open for a second in disbelief, and all I could reply with was—" Oh!"

He told me to contact the center on another frequency; the controller on the new frequency told me to turn 20 degrees left and to vacate flight level 410 for 280; then he asked what rate of descent I could give him. I said we had a plane full of passengers and was giving him 3,000 feet per minute, but if necessary I could double or triple that amount. There was a long pause—he must have been on the "land line" with the next controller—and when he came back he said, "Roger 200 Tango Whiskey, turn right direct Nottingham and rejoin the DuPont four, descend to and maintain Flight Level two two zero."

So, just as fast as things had gone haywire things were becoming normal again. In a Learjet, with a horrendous tail wind we're covering ten miles per minute and stuff happens very quickly. The rest of the trip from there was a lot of descending and turning; twelve minutes after crossing OTT we were clearing runway 29 at 40 N, and my work day was over—or so I thought.

My director of operations was on the Unicom frequency as I cleared 29; he told me of a predicament our company was in. It seems we had a King Air trip booked from home to Northeast Philly for a pick-up there, and then over to Morgantown, West Virginia to take a mom and dad and their three children on a skiing trip, drop them off and return home empty. However, the King Air would not start, so he had called another Lear crew in to fly our Lear 36, but they had had a hydraulic issue with it, so they could not fly that plane either. But, here I was and they wondered if I could 'do' the trip with this plane.

"Certainly, most definitely," was my reply. I deplaned our four Orlando people and their baggage just as the sun was setting and the ice-cold polar winds howled out of the west at 30 knots.

I started transferring fuel to the trunk and then I ordered from our fuel guy, Eric, a top off of Jet A with prist; also a ground power cart in order to conserve my very limited battery power. I grabbed the paperwork as the D.O. filed my flight plans, and fifteen minutes later we blasted off for PNE under visual flight rules and asked Philly approach for a clearance into their Class Bravo airspace.

This ended with a landing on Northeast's runway 33 after a quick twelve-minute trip as opposed to a twenty-five-minute Instrument Flight Rule gig. After explaining our company's sick airplane woes to a very understanding family, I told the dad we'd have him there in forty minutes and that my company had an awaiting stretched limousine as opposed to his rental car, as this was the least we could do since they would be a good hour late.

He was very appreciative and also very excited about taking the trip in a Lear instead of the King Air he was paying for ! We actually had to wait on them for fifteen minutes while they used rest rooms, gathered up the kids, and so on. Finally, at 5:45 p.m. we were once again turning money into noise.

En route, I studied the airport diagrams, approaches, and called Flight Service for current runway conditions— known to pilots as Notices to Airmen. My concerns were a combination of several issues. Morgantown has a north-south runway and the winds there were from the west at 22 knots with gusts to 32. Also, the runway length was 5,000 feet which is the shortest I will personally fly into with a Lear 35. However, the runway reportedly had accumulations of packed snow and ice, but no braking action reports were available.

Hmmm—seems like this could get very interesting. With winds as such and with my fuel load, my final approach speed would have to be 135 knots, and the landing distance charts say I'll use 3,000 feet of real estate to stop in. These charts are based on weight, so if we are adding any speed at all to these figures for wind and wind gusts, we have to keep adding to the amount of runway required. Throw in a contaminated runway and you keep adding feet required. Throw in a contaminated runway without a braking action report and keep adding. These were a few of my thoughts as we descended into the West Virginia night's turbulent air.

After breaking through the 2,000-foot-thick icy cloud cover we were cleared for the visual to runway 18, and everything I had briefed with Charlie went according to plan. My short field approach and maximum braking effort resulted in another well planned adventure.

About twenty minutes after delivering our passengers into their waiting limo we were heading for Harrisburg to join up with the Bunts One arrival corridor into Philly. We sweet-talked Air Traffic Control into a few short cuts and thirty minutes after departing Morgantown we were once again back home safe and sound.

Charlie started cleaning up the cabin and getting our luggage out of the plane while I finished the shut-down checks. Some of the most rewarding times of a work day for me are these checks. Upon shutting off the inverters and batteries, the gyros keep whining for five minutes in a tone that I always enjoy to hear.

As these gyros continued their ever so slowing serenade I sat there with my eyes closed and hands gripping the yoke, savoring a well-known feeling. It's a feeling that only happens at the end of a challenging flight. It's a feeling that's very hard for me to put into words. Here I am sitting in the dark with an unwinding mechanical marvel, with feelings as though the plane is almost human; or are they feelings as though I am almost mechanical ? Whichever is the case, tonight I know the plane and I had been 'one'. We had been through a lot and we came out as predicted. She did not let me down and I came through for her.

It's almost the same feeling I used to get on the farm when shutting down the last tractor for the night after successfully milking 110 cows twice that day and baling 1,600 bales of hay. I acknowledge that I am so lucky to have a job that is so satisfying to me. And I also thank God each and every day that he continues to give me the strength to enjoy my life. A life which includes one of the greatest jobs on earth—the life of a Learjet Captain !

54.   SHUTTLE TRAINING

On a recent pop-up trip last Saturday afternoon I had yet another experience worth sharing with you. It's such an unusual event, I'll bet you have never read about anything similar.

I had gotten up at 5 a.m. on Saturday to attend around twenty of our community garage sales here in New Holland, Pennsylvania. I love to find these deals, but my wife hates me to bring other people's junk home! It was a rainy day, and by noon I had walked my usual two miles and was soaked to the hide. I returned to my apartment and was cleaning up when the phone call came. I was to fly into Dulles to pick up two passengers, depart at 5 p.m. local and fly them to SNA (Santa Anna, California— John Wayne Field in Orange County, home of the World Champion Anaheim Angels.)

The weather was pea soup with Dulles Automatic Terminal Information Service calling overcast sky at 600 feet with one mile visibility in heavy rain. Off we blasted with our trusty Lear 31A for the twenty-five-minute low altitude flight southbound. The radar told the story well, showing clusters of green and yellow and an occasional red blob thrown in for scary measures. While being vectored on the right downwind for the ILS to 35 Right, the ATIS was still calling 600 overhead and one mile visibility, no problem, right? Wrong!

The pilot not flying was calling altitudes to decision height by the hundreds to go, until I vividly remember him calling: "200 feet to go; 100 feet to go; okay, you're at decision height, I don't see anything—Oh, no wait, there's the lead in lights—continue; runway is in sight; fence checks, three green and we are cleared to land." And land we did. I remember braking quite gingerly just to make sure we had brakes and the anti-skid system releasing my inputs, and that's how I judge rainfall. If the anti-skid braking system keeps releasing my foot pressure, we probably are plowing through a half-inch of water standing on the runway!

We refueled, loaded up Mr. And Mrs. Big, and off we climbed through the westbound clouds, rain and turbulence. I remember not turning off the fasten seatbelt sign until we were through 34,000 feet. It was a rough ride until we broke out of the tops around 33,000 feet. I usually turn off the sign when climbing through 10,000 feet if it's a smooth ride. We coped with 100-knot head winds for the bulk of the first leg into GRI (Grand Island, Nebraska) my selected fuel stop.

The major airline carriers do all the flight planning for their Captains, but that's not the case for us—we are Federal Aviation Regulations Part 135 guys—we have to plan it all, from flight planning, to where I want to stop for fuel, to where I need to divert to if the weather is down at my destination. I have to plan everything. Grand Island is a remote area with great friendly service and cheap fuel. When I called them before departing our home base at 40 N, I told them I'd like a ground power unit, a quick-turn top-off of jet A negative prist— and two turkey and Swiss cheese box lunches for us two drivers.

They were ready. A mere twenty minutes after shutting down the big Garretts we were once again turning money into noise. However I need to tell you right now of my first ever power-to-idle arrival and landing.

We were 100 miles out from GRI when I told Air Traffic Control that I needed lower—and **now**! He had forgotten to turn us over to the next sector, and when I checked in with them, the controller was somewhat slow to issue our next clearance, but finally we were cleared to 23,000 feet. By now we were only 70 miles out and still at 43,000 feet! I slowly reduced thrust to flight idle as we picked our way through the descent, and then the approach check lists. I extended the spoilers and trimmed the plane for 250 knots. The vertical speed indicator read 6,000 feet per minute descent rate. I dropped through a broken layer cloud bank to see the airport quite directly beneath us.

A few "S" turns were needed, and ten minutes after idling the engines we greased the five Goodyears onto the 59-degree Nebraska tarmac. I had never touched the throttles once from 43,000 feet! How's that for minute planning?

The next afternoon we departed SNA and headed back for Dulles with my planned fuel stop in Salina, Kansas. The winds aloft and weather made me want to refuel there. Again, as I was about 100 miles from there, Air Traffic Control said I could descend immediately if I took an off-course vector, but if I kept flying direct I would need to stay at 43,000 feet for another 15 miles. "Hang 'em high," I told the pilot not flying; he in turn relayed the message to Control that we would stay high.

It seemed we were in for another space shuttle approach, only this one became even more interesting. At 70 miles out we were cleared on down, and again the thrust levers were cautiously pulled back to flight idle. The spoilers were extended, and down we floated almost weightlessly while busily working on completing all our checklists in eight-and-a-half minutes. The difference this time from the previous afternoon's approach was that we had an 80-knot tail wind booting us faster towards our destination runway. At 520 knots across the ground, real estate slides past around 10 percent faster than it does with no tail wind, and over maybe 20 percent faster than when with a head wind !

I requested and was granted the same "S" turns as I had done the day before, but still when I turned the four-mile final and had fully configured the great white jet for landing, I remember thinking there was no way José that we could lose enough altitude in order to land straight in, so it was now time for one last trick.

I over-rode my Yaw Dampening Computer and its servo system by lowering the left wing somewhat while pushing the right rudder so as to slip the plane through the air sideways, creating increased drag which in turn helps decrease an airplane's flying performance. For the next three miles the cockpit was very quiet.

If I could not land on the first 1,000 feet I would simply add power and circle for a normal power-on approach. This was certainly an ideal set up for unusual flight circumstances. You never know—some day when both Garrett Turbofans become ghostly silent, I may need to rely on these past two days' experiences! (Otherwise known as money in the bank !)

Anyway, while on the last one-mile final and still slipping, I knew things were looking rather perfect, so I took away the slip, pitched the jet for a speed of V Ref plus 20 knots (135 knots), flared, landed at 115 knots, and held her nose high so as to decelerate while using only aerodynamic drag—saving the mechanical brakes for the next landing.

Picture perfect ! An artist at work ! I wonder how many people were watching ? Aw, it really doesn't matter; I have that baby tucked away in under my belt forever anyway. Another "for real" power-off from a 43,000 feet high descent, approach and landing completed !

As we cleared the runway, Tower said they were naming this arrival "The Number One shuttle approach of the decade !"

I keyed the mike and replied, "Yeah, we were just practicing for our future upgrade Space Shuttle training ! "

(Just a note here: All pilots are taught these emergency glides but it is only in the *uncongested, uncontested* Midwest that a high performance jet driver can actually practice such evasive maneuvers.)

55. Into Pierre Again

Yesterday's morning chores started early for Pat and I. We met at 40N around 5:45 am and it was a brisk November morning with the temps hovering around freezing. Our jet for this three-day excursion would be N200TW, a Lear 35A that Brian Fisher had just pulled out of our new hangar which we call the Taj Mahal. I met Brian in the terminal building when I stopped in to grab a hot cup of coffee; I told him to go ahead and start filling the wings and tips and that I would also need a ground power unit too because I would be transferring fuel into our trunk tank.

When I arrived planeside everything was in progress. I loaded my suitcase and computer into the rear storage compartment and then jumped up front into my front office. I flipped on the battery switches and began the fuel transfer. While I would be there for a few minutes pumping 600 pounds into the trunk I also completed all of the cockpit preflighting checks. Partway through all of this commotion Patrick arrived. We said our usual 'hello how are you' things and he then preflighted the exterior. I have only worked with Pat for a few weeks now but we get along very well with similar personalities and work ethics. What is amazing to me is that with all this excitement of flying the world's sleekest jets, what it all really boils down to is the satisfaction of working with other really neat people and enjoying the unshakable bonds that are established between crew members. Don't get me wrong; flying Learjets and getting paid to do so is a very cool deal but in the end working with and helping others rules my world.

Our instrument approach charts and plates had expired so I loaded all of the old ones into my car and Pat replaced Tango Whiskey's cupboards with the new ones. US Terminal Procedure Charts as well as the High and Low Altitude Charts (instrument airway maps) are good for eight weeks and then get replaced with new ones.

Soon I was on the computer logged in at my company's pilot planning room filling out my flight logs, weight and balance papers as well as printing out my filed flight plans, weather forecasts and notices to airmen for my arrival airports and for the alternate airports as well. Around 10 minutes to seven Pat closed the hatch and we were ready to get going.

He flew the first leg to Teterboro, New Jersey. Our clearance from Philadelphia Clearance Delivery was: after entering controlled airspace to fly direct to the Modena VOR, then track Victor 3 to the Solberg VOR, then direct to the field. With our radios all set for this initial clearance and the preflight checks completed we once again started turning money into noise. Pat taxied to runway 11 as he and I both worked through the taxiing checks together. Then

I called Philly departure on my cell phone and received our release.

Departing runway 11 at 7 am on a clear November fall day you will see hardly anything out the front windscreen except for the sun. Pat and I had discussed this issue prior to taxiing and I had suggested that as we were climbing away from the airport towards Modena that we climb to the south of the arrival course to runway 29. We are always concerned about the danger of hitting other airplanes that may be arriving in from the opposite direction while we are departing, especially when there is no wind. Chester County Airport is 'uncontrolled airspace' and there can always be small airplanes flying around with no radios and hence no audible clue as to their whereabouts. Visual clues are about all we have when departing such airspace. As soon as we were climbing and finishing after-takeoff checks, I checked in with Philly Departure and we were told to fly a heading of 90 degrees and to expect direct Solberg very soon.

Before long we were cleared to 11,000 feet direct SBJ. The morning's air and views were splendid. Teterboro's ATIS called winds light and variable and said to expect the VOR Alpha instrument approach. I had begun pumping fuel into the trunk as soon as practical after take-off as we were going to leave TEB with maximum fuel for our three-and-a half-hour flight to Pierre, South Dakota. Soon we flew direct Wanes and were cleared for the approach three miles outside of Wanes. Stepping down inbound on the TEB 125 degree radial we crossed Jaymo at 2,000 and then Clifo at 1,500 feet with the airport in sight. We were told to enter left traffic for runway 19 and we were cleared to land by the tower as we turned downwind. Pat flew a perfect approach and greased her onto terra firma and exited at the end. Soon we were on Jet Avitat's ramp filling up with more fuel with a GPU giving us the needed 28 volt DC auxiliary power. I ordered newspapers, regular coffee and a bag of ice for the cooler. In twenty minutes time we were ready for our passenger, his dog, and the next leg to PIR.

With Tom , Abbey and all of the luggage onboard we taxied to runway 24 as I marveled at the new taxiways they have built at TEB. Construction has been going on there seemingly forever but the outcome is phenomenal. Beautiful new taxiways and rebuilt older ones all ease the flow and prevent congestion. If any airport needed help with congestion it surely was Teterboro. We departed runway 24 executing the Teterboro Five departure procedure which has us fly runway heading to 1,500 feet and then a right turn to 280 degrees while maintaining 1,500 feet until we are 4.5 miles from the field at which time we climb to 2,000 feet while maintaining that same heading.

After a few New York Departure vectors we were cleared direct Coate, then Lake Henry, then Dunkirk and then direct Pierre. Some days just seem to flow while others it seems we have to fight tooth and nail to get anything done. This flight went silky smooth coming out of the Big Apple. It seemed every time we were approaching a clearance altitude we were given a higher altitude so that we never had to level off, and it's that levelling off that is usually the norm departing the busiest airspace in the world.

The last clearance we received while climbing through 19,000 feet was to our filed altitude of 40,000 feet. As I leveled the great white jet at flight level 400, I remarked to Pat that we had burned 800 pounds of fuel so far in the first twenty minutes of this flight. The outside air temperature at FL400 was a frigid minus 72 degrees Celsius. Very soon our Mach meter was showing 0.78. Power was set to 795 degrees centigrade per side and life was good.

Around the Cleveland to Detroit area we crossed a 200 mile wide cold front with its associated light to moderate turbulence. Also around this time I began pumping fuel forward into the wings from the trunk compartment. I usually wait until each tip tank is down to 500 pounds which proves to me the tip jet pumps are working as they should. By the time our trip clock said two hours we were feet wet over Lake Michigan with the fuel transfer completed. Milwaukee then slipped by us maybe fifty miles to our south. Next came Wisconsin and then the Moline VOR at Quad Cities. Soon thereafter Patrick was busy collecting weather at Pierre as well as checking on Tom's rendezvous vehicle. Just as smoothly as this whole day was going, all was well and in place at Pierre with no surprises in sight.

At 200 miles out from our destination we were told to descend to 34,000 feet and shortly after that we were told 32,000 feet with our discretion to 24,000 feet. As I leveled the ship at FL 320 I turned on our engine nacelle heat to begin warming the intakes. We had an undercast between us and PIR which meant icing conditions. At this time I noticed the outside air temperature was still a chilly minus 52 degrees. As the miles were ticking away I started my descent out of 32,000 feet at 120 miles out from PIR and also turned on the wing and stab anti-ice. Settling into a nice 2,500 feet per minute descent we entered the clouds at 28,000 feet as Pat was again checking PIR's weather for any changes. As we vacated 24,000 feet the next controller cleared us to 5,000 feet and told us to call the field when we had it in sight.

Pat at this point set both of our HISs for the ILS 31 as I navigated towards the airport using my GPS and heading bug. I remember being fifty miles out and descending through 22,000 feet which suited me just fine. Believe me after being so used to flying in congested airspace it is a pleasure to receive these South Dakota clearances which seem to allow us to do almost whatever we want to do. Soon we were twenty miles away from our destination and were descending out of the thick clouds through 10,000 feet. Ground contact was visually confirmed by Pat and by the time we were settling at 5,000 feet we could indeed see we were over pheasant country ! Pat called the field in sight at eight miles out and we were cleared for the visual approach into Pierre. We then cancelled IFR with Center as I maneuvered towards the south of the field for runway 31. There was some freezing rain and snow in the air so I left all of our anti-icing switches on.

I was still a little high and fast at five miles out so up came the spoilers and back came the pitch trim button. At 170 knots I stowed the boards and called for approach flaps. I then turned a three mile final and asked Pat for flaps 20, gear down and landing checks. At 1.5 miles out I called for landing flaps and soon we were clearing runway 31 onto Capital City Air Charter's ramp. I followed the tug around a Citation jet and then shut down.

We deplaned and loaded all of Tom's possessions into his awaiting SUV. Abbey, the black lab, was so anxious to get off the jet I had to hold her back until the steps were down and then help her down to the tarmac. After 3.3 hours of flying against a 110 knot headwind, I can't blame the dog for wanting to stand on the ground and to find the nearest bush. After some more chatting with Tom, he and his pheasant hunting guides departed while Pat and I began unloading our luggage as well as securing the jet for a three-day layover. Now that the work for this day was completed it was time for us to explore Pierre, South Dakota once again. I'll take this job over a factory job any day, thank you !

56. Mentor Flight

Yesterday I had the pleasure of working once again with the man who taught me all of my ratings, Captain Ken Kamp. We flew from home base to Farmingdale (FRG) at 7:30 a.m. to pick up four members of Summit Aviation and bring them back to Coatesville (40N) for the first board meeting of our new company, JetDirect Aviation. Later in the afternoon Ken and I flew the trip again and returned the guys back to their home base; then we flew back to 40N empty.

These kinds of round robin trips are really fun for both of us because we are both seasoned Captains, and usually Captains don't get to fly with each other, let alone the student (me) and mentor (Ken) issue. Ken had been my mentor; he taught me all my ratings, from my very first rating as Private Pilot in 1993 to all my subsequent Instructor ratings. It was also really cool, while taxiing, to think that the combined total Learjet experience sitting in these two front seats easily exceeded 10,000 hours.

But one point today was driven home to me: that the potential danger of mid-air collisions actually can *increase* when weather conditions improve. Let me explain how and why this can happen.

We were fogged in when we departed Coatesville in the morning. Ken flew the first leg, and by the time we shot the ILS 14 at Farmingdale that airport also was fogged in, but no problem, Ken nailed that circling approach. The four men were waiting; they climbed in; we turned around and headed back to Coatesville and the board meeting. I was flying the return leg.

I departed FRG with a forward visibility of maybe 600 feet. I hand flew just about the whole flight and also hand flew the ILS 29 back in to 40N. Nailed it too.

By afternoon the weather cleared dramatically. When we returned the guys to Farmingdale visibilities in the whole northeast were up to four miles so we ended up doing visual approaches. As usual the most dangerous minutes of every day for me on a round robin trip are landing back at 40N without having a mid-air collision with the many small general aviation airplanes. They are numerous. Our field has no tower and we need one. Another factor each afternoon is arriving into the 40N area from the east with the sun in our eyes. Last night there was a pesky layer of haze from 5,000 feet down to 2,500 feet. Flying westbound into this is so stressful, especially when we get maybe 10 miles from home. At that point we cancel IFR so that we can switch our radios to the local traffic frequency of 122.7; and about then is when Philly Approach warns us of many local targets showing up on their radar screen in front of us.

It is a time when every nanosecond is spent defending our lives, believe me. The big sky, little airplane theory doesn't hold squat with me. I have had more than a few 'near misses' both here and at other uncontrolled fields over the past six years, and each one is one too many for me. Last night the planes were landing on runway 11 so Ken and I felt an ILS to runway 29 might interfere with their departure paths. Some guys were doing practice ILS to 29 so there were small planes everywhere going in every direction. At times like this there is no real correct answer as to which runway we should land on. We slow down to 160 knots and enter the pattern the best way we see fit, based on the activity at the current time. Last night we entered on a midfield crosswind for 11. As I announced this another guy said he was on a downwind for 11 also. Thank God we fly a 1,500 foot pattern and the little guys fly an 800 footer. We finally saw him below us and we extended our downwind and he kept his in tight. But let me assure you when we turned left downwind and into that setting sun in the haze layer the visibility was really poor. I just pray as I look and announce our turn that we do not hit a small plane flying around with no radio.

Thirty seconds after turning base we were clearing runway 11 and the day's adventures were history. High stress time was over for another day. I feel, and we actually are, much more safe and secure when the weather is poor back home here in Coatesville. Like yesterday morning when I hand flew our ILS 29 to almost minimums: Because of the fog, there had been no other airplanes (no small craft) landing at 40N when we had departed two hours earlier. I believe this is why most mid-air accidents happen on beautiful, sunny and clear days. Oh well, another day in paradise and another dollar well earned while working together with my friend and mentor, Ken Kamp.

56. Drawing the Line

While taxiing to runway 29 last evening, I was briefing Charlie Dog as to our departure clearance out of Chester County, followed by our in-flight emergency plans.

"I will execute a short-field static run-up and departure from runway 29 and you will say our normal call-outs. You or I can call and I will initiate an abort before our V1 take off decision speed of 115 knots, but after that I will fly the airplane and you will help me with any abnormal checklists and radio calls. I will turn to a heading of 260 degrees at 1,100 feet for the local noise abatement procedures. After passing through 1,600 feet I will turn right, right turn to Modena (MXE) and will level at 3,000 feet. There is a major cluster of thunderstorms within a stone's throw of that fix, so I am planning on deviating to the left, or north of there if needed. Are there any questions Charlie Dog ?"

"Sounds like a plan to me Captain," he said . The standard departure from 40 N's 29 is a left turn to MXE, so when I brief anything to the contrary such as the non-standard right turn, I always say the direction twice. *Twice.* Once my turn was enough that my radar could paint Modena, I could hardly believe the monster storms that I was looking at on the scope. Philly had warned us as we picked up our IFR release that all out-bound PHL traffic had been stopped due to this fast approaching line and clusters of thunderstorms.

"Lear 156 Juliet Sierra, radar contact two miles north of the County; fly heading of 100 degrees and intercept Victor 3; climb now and maintain 4,000."

Isn't it funny that I can sit here right now and hear that controller's voice just as clear as it was sixteen hours ago ? I can even recall smaller details like how I kept bugging C. Dog to get us higher for a smoother ride and also, how I can still see all of those bright red cotton-ball-sized radar echoes on our radar screen that we had to deviate around on our twenty-four minute low-altitude 250-knot flight on up to Teterboro. We were flying generally into better weather but still had to fly the ILS 19 approach into TEB. The instrument landing glide slope was unusable so we stepped our way down in altitude by increments onto the 7,000 foot long runway.

We were to pick up a doctor and fly her to Cleveland tonight. Once shut down and inside Atlantic Aviation's flight planning room, I kept hearing that line from the Eagles hit song, *Lyin Eyes*—"another night, it's gonna' be a long one"....

The pick-up started out as usual: Fresh ice, coffee, newspapers and some more kerosene for our bird. I called for and received my clearance about twenty-eight minutes prior to our 9:30 departure time. After I read it back to the controller for verification, I asked if we could expect any delays.

"Oh yeah," is all he said at first, but then he also told me to call for an update at 10:00.

I then relayed that message to Charlie Dog and to dispatch. At 10:00 we were told to call back at 10:30. You see, when severe weather is moving through, things change by the minute. It's kind of like playing a basketball game. Every time the ball is thrown to another player, the whole situation changes as well as the options. It seems I was on the flight planning computer getting updates every ten minutes, then back out to the jet calling Air Traffic Control for updates. Every time that I had an update from ATC, I would also call dispatch to keep them informed of the new development. I spoke with a senior US Airways Captain for a spell during one of my briefing room visits while we each sat side by side staring glumly at the radar screens. He was flying a Canada Air Regional Jet with about thirty passengers and they were trying to get to Washington's Dulles airport. He showed me his escape plan and then I showed him mine.

Like I said, things changed every minute. I would hear a jet depart and wondered where he might be going. One thing was for certain—the way the radar returns looked to me, I had to leave soon or I'd be sitting for another three hours. I called ground control again at 10:30 and he told me to call clearance as they had a revision to my flight plan. I called them and son-of-a-gun if they didn't give me the routing which I had told the US Airways guy I thought would work.

After that I called ground control back and he said to start the engines. I ran into the FBO and got the Doc and the Dog. Lightning was flashing relentlessly. We had very

poor visibilities while taxiing to runway 24. Upon nearing
the run-up parking area, I saw we were maybe tenth in line
for take-off. Everyone parked their anxious jets off to the
side and, whenever an exit gate would open, ATC would
release whoever was next in turn that was heading in that
direction.

As we parked facing towards the southwest, I could see
a monstrous cluster of thunderstorms on the radar scope
moving our way. Thirty minutes later it was raining so hard
with lightning everywhere that I said to the Dog I didn't
think we should just sit here burning fuel. The issue at
hand wasn't so much whether we waited in the running jet
or whether we waited inside but that inside I could at least
keep up with the changing conditions on the computer's
current radar page. We not only had to deal with the weather
for our TEB departure but also there was a nasty 300-mile-
long north-to-south line that had just moved through our
destination area and was heading our way; that had to be
dealt with on our descent.

We called ground control to return to the FBO and it
was the most difficult five-minute taxi of my career. The
rain fell in buckets as I simply crawled at a snail's pace to
the FBO because we could not see very well. I shut down
the engines and a lineman stood here with an umbrella as
we opened the door. As I tip-toed towards the building
under the umbrella the water was up to my ankles ! I checked
the radar and made a quick decision. I was simply not going
to fly for another two hours as the whole metropolitan area
was getting hammered.

I ran back to the plane through all that water again to
tell Charlie Dog and the Doc of my decision. Charlie had
to run in to hit the head so I was to tell the Doc of my new
plan.

I said, "Maam... Maam...Maam," but she was sleeping so soundly that she did not hear me. I called a few more times getting louder with each breath. She was in a semi-reclined position on the rear divan with her feet up on the seat in front of her, as in a Lazy Boy chair, and I wondered—should I just grab her shoe and wiggle it a little?

I called ground control again and told them to cancel my clearance, that it would be another hour or two before things looked better to me. "Roger that Six Juliet Sierra, that's a good decision; New York has just closed all west-bound gates again anyway."

I slithered back into a mid-cabin seat and kept calling the Doc with more and more forceful tones each time until finally, as I was running out of wind, her eyes opened into a semi-conscious state. It was then I told her that I was drawing the line and that we were going to wait for an hour or two inside.

She was very concerned of a meeting that she absolutely needed to attend at 8 a.m. in Cleveland the next morning and that was the reason she had hired a private jet to get her home tonight in the first place. I assured her that as soon as it was safe I would get her home, but for now there was no way I was going to fly, for safety reasons. As she continued to awaken she realized that my decision was based solely on safety and that she didn't want to do anything risky either. So we tip-toed back inside the terminal under a huge two-man (woman, person?) umbrella through the still over two-inch-deep water that kept on falling but had no place to flow.

I took her in to see what was on our flight planning computers as far as the radar returns. She took one look at the computer screen and said, "Oh my God, what are all these yellow and red colors ?"

I explained that they were thunderstorm cells. Then I found her a nice corner in a quiet pilot rest room and even found her a blanket. She thanked me but seemed more concerned that I try to get some sleep too ! It was by now midnight.

I then called dispatch and told them also of the new plan. Around 1:00 a.m. I refiled two new flight plans, rechecked all current and forecast weather conditions, and headed back out into the rain. Clearance issued us a new deal and off we taxied towards the foggy and rainy departure end of runway 24—hopefully the last time tonight!

We departed in moderate rain which lasted for fifty miles or so. By the time we were past Allentown and above 25,000 feet the night time beauty of flying jets finally made me feel good again. We had had our share of problems tonight but by God look how beautiful that big old moon looks right outside my window now! I think I can just reach out there and touch it!

Every inbound Airliner it seems was given holding instructions as Newark, La Guardia and Kennedy were still backed up considerably. I remember feeling sorry for those pilots as the holding process increases the work load on an already busy arrival, but the main issue on my mind was now getting the Doc home.

Temps and dew point spreads were even at 22 degrees at Cleveland's Hopkins and Lakefront airports but our Cuyahoga Falls airport had not reported for the past two hours for some unknown reason, so I had to wait until on our descent to get their current conditions.

Before we left TEB I knew I could get into Burke (BKL) or Hopkins (CLE) as they both had ILSs to 200 feet and a half-mile visibility, and the weather was reported to be 300 and 1 which is above minimums . We diverted our way through the fifty-mile-wide frontal weather system over western Pennsylvania and lucked out with only light to an occasional moderate bump.

Cleveland Approach finally reported the Cayuhoga Falls (CGF) weather to us when asked; it seemed their ILS 24 would work. We were still 10,000 feet too high when the last controller gave us a heading for the intercept. As we turned for the intercept we blew right through the final approach course. I asked the kind of rude-sounding controller for vectors around again and, four minutes later when properly slowed and level at 3,000 feet, the localizer was captured, and inbound we flew in hopes of seeing a bright awaiting runway.

Fully configured for landing at the 5.8 mile outer marker final approach fix, we captured the glide slope and vacated 3,000 feet for 1,079 feet (otherwise known as decision height—that is, 200 feet above the ground). When arriving there you're either going to see a runway and land on it, or you are not going to see the runway and execute the published missed approach—in plain English, "Get the heck back up and out of there while following a planned escape route."

I told Charlie to click the transmitter on the tower frequency seven times to turn on the runway lights as we passed the marker and to start our time in case we lost the glide slope. Again, at two miles out I asked him to reclick the transmitter just in case; after he did that again, I clicked my transmitter seven times also for good measure. When the tower closes for the night it is up to us plane drivers to activate the airport's lighting ourselves. Usually seven clicks on the tower frequency will turn all of the runway lights on high intensity; five clicks for medium, and three for low intensity.

Finally, at 300 feet above the ground—just like snapping your thumbs, a beautiful runway appeared in front of us . At fifty feet the lights were so blinding to me that I keyed the mike three times; the lights instantly faded to low intensity as the great white jet greased onto terra firma so delicately that one could not tell when the Goodyears kissed the blacktop.

Our Lady of the evening was now awake and very enthusiastic for the first time all night. I shut down the jet and was helping her off the plane just as her awaiting limo arrived alongside the plane. She thanked us maybe five times in the next minute or so for what she termed our professional, friendly, and safe service, and off they disappeared into the misty and foggy 3 a.m. Cleveland darkness.

I ordered a power cart and 160 gallons of go-juice, then went inside to see if there was any way we would get back home. Surprisingly, the weather was not that bad at Philly, Reading, Lancaster or Wilmington. Those airports are the ones that we use when returning to 40 N as they're big enough airports to have weather reports and close enough to home so that we may get some idea what to expect weather-wise. In the 25 or so minutes we were there, quite a fog bank had formed; I think the visibility was around a half-mile when we left. The ride was nice and relaxing for the last leg as we shot the ILS to 29 back home to about 600 and 2 (at 600 feet above the ground we broke out of the clouds and could see two miles in front of us).

Once again as the great white flying machine was winding down on the Coatesville ramp, I couldn't help chuckling to myself as I thought of the events of this evening. We should have been home and finished up well before midnight. It was now 4 a.m. and I had another half-hour of paper work to do and still a forty-minute drive to my house after that. All the plans for my next four-day western gig were for naught; I would have to give up that trip because it would be starting well before my ten hours of mandatory rest was over.

Oh well, I was home, I was in one piece, I had drawn the line, but then I had delivered the goods . Safely delivered the goods. I was not bored with my job. Not bored at all. I was tired to the bone but I was not bored. And I had stashed yet another night full of experiences in under my belt. Just like money in the bank, as they say. I guess you can't ask any more than that from your job !